TALKING
UNTIL
NIGHTFALL

TALKING UNTIL NIGHTFALL

Remembering Jewish Salonica 1941–44

ISAAC MATARASSO

Translated and introduced by
Pauline Matarasso

With contributions by
Robert Matarasso and François Matarasso

BLOOMSBURY CONTINUUM
LONDON · OXFORD · NEW YORK · NEW DELHI · SYDNEY

BLOOMSBURY CONTINUUM
Bloomsbury Publishing Plc
50 Bedford Square, London, WC1B 3DP, UK

BLOOMSBURY, BLOOMSBURY CONTINUUM and the Diana logo are trademarks
of Bloomsbury Publishing Plc

First published in Great Britain 2020

Dedicated to the memory of
Isaac Matarasso (1892–1958)
Robert Matarasso (1927–1982)
and the entire Jewish community of Salonica
who suffered under the Occupation (1941–44)

'For the dead and the living, we must bear witness.'
Elie Wiesel

CONTENTS

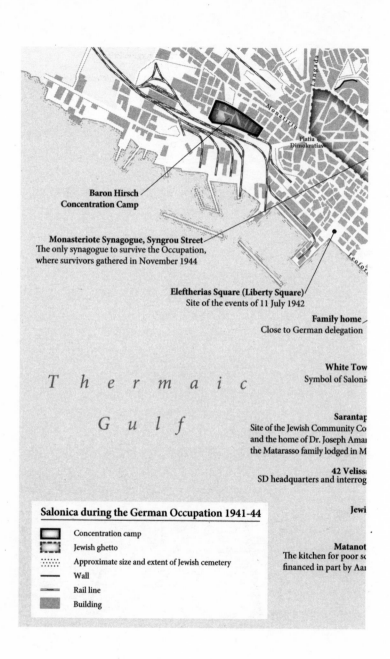

Baron Hirsch
Concentration Camp

Monasteriote Synagogue, Syngrou Street
The only synagogue to survive the Occupation,
where survivors gathered in November 1944

Eleftherias Square (Liberty Square)
Site of the events of 11 July 1942

Family home
Close to German delegation

White Tow
Symbol of Saloni

Sarantap
Site of the Jewish Community Co
and the home of Dr. Joseph Amar
the Matarasso family lodged in M

42 Veliss
SD headquarters and interrog

Jewi

Matanot
The kitchen for poor s
financed in part by Aar

T h e r m a i c

G u l f

Platia
Dimokratias

Salonica during the German Occupation 1941-44

▭	Concentration camp
▨	Jewish ghetto
⋮⋮	Approximate size and extent of Jewish cemetery
—	Wall
▭	Rail line
▨	Building

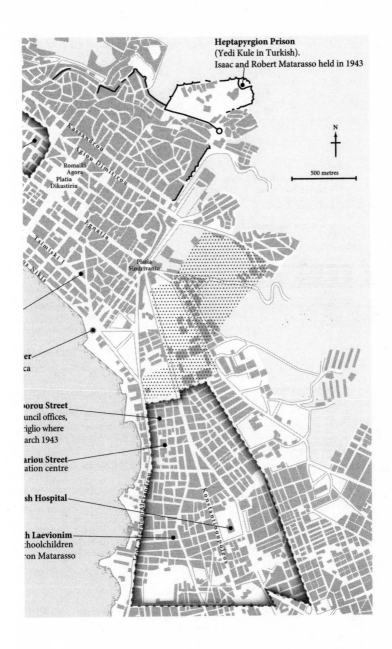

Heptapyrgion Prison
(Yedi Kule in Turkish).
Isaac and Robert Matarasso held in 1943

N

500 metres

Kassandrou

Agiou Dimitriou

Romaiki
Agora
Platia
Dikastiriu

Egnatia

Tsimiski

os Nikis

Platia
Sindrivaniu

Konstantinoupoleos

Vasilissis Olgas/Alatini?

...er
...ca

...porou Street
...uncil offices,
...riglio where
...arch 1943

...ariou Street
...ation centre

...sh Hospital

...h Laevionim
...choolchildren
...ron Matarasso

Foreword: Remembering the Witnesses

Can there be anything left to say about the Shoah? Surely every story has been heard, every angle covered, every opinion expressed. And yet, time passes. Those who survived, who saw and witnessed, are reaching the natural term of their lives. New generations inherit the bad with the good. They need to know what happened, because it did. It is not necessary to say anything new about these events. It is necessary only to say it again, like a prayer, not because it makes something happen, but because it might change us.

This book gathers the testimony of witnesses, and of those who knew them: three generations of a family. Isaac Matarasso (1892–1958) and his son, Robert (1927–1982), survived the German occupation of Salonica (Thessaloniki, in Greece) and the almost complete destruction of an ancient Jewish community. Isaac (IM) was a doctor and took an active part in the community's social services and cultural life. He made notes as events took place and wrote a full record after the Liberation, submitting his reports (in French) to relief agencies, and publishing articles (in Greek) in the newly revived Jewish press. Most of this material was collected into a small volume, published as . . . *And Yet Not All Died* . . . in Athens in September 1948. It was the first account of the Shoah available in Greek, and that text, newly translated by his daughter-in-law from IM's original French, forms the centre of this book (Part III).

The report is striking in its objective tone, as the writer places himself in the service of his community and almost 50,000 murdered co-religionists. He and his extended family make no appearance: this is a collective experience. But Isaac Matarasso also wrote some much more personal pieces, tributes to friends he had lost and glimpses of life under Nazi brutality, which reveal other facets of his attractive, principled character. They were not published in his lifetime, appearing in French Jewish periodicals only after his death. These are published here in English for the first time and comprise Part IV.

Robert Matarasso (RM), the only child of Isaac and his French wife, Andreé, was 14 when the German army took Salonica in April 1941; he was 17 when they left. By then, he had witnessed terrible things, including the ghetto, deportations, prison, and months with the Greek Resistance, separated from his parents. He was lucky to be alive. The city in which he had spent a happy childhood, the community where he felt at home, were gone. The reunited family moved to Athens in the spring of 1946, and he subsequently left for Paris to escape the Greek Civil War. In 1953 he married Pauline (*née* Sanderson), and later they moved to England. In his early fifties he began to write a memoir of his wartime experiences, but he died suddenly, without completing it. Extracts from that document, written in English and introduced by his widow, are included as Part V.

Pauline Matarasso (b. 1929) knew IM during the last ten years of his life, and formed a deep bond with her father-in-law, who had seen so much but kept faith with humanity. She has written a biographical introduction, drawing on her recollections, family letters and other sources. A translator and historian, she has prepared all the English versions of the French texts. Her affectionate portrait of Isaac Matarasso opens the book as Part I.

It is followed, in Part II, by a short text in which IM recalls his life as a medical student in France before and during the First World War, when he met Andrée (*née* Rey), whom he married and brought home to Salonica, and whose Catholic origins would play a part in the family's survival. Written towards the end of his life, this meditative sketch evokes a happier time before the catastrophe of the Nazi occupation and so makes an appropriate overture.

François Matarasso (b. 1958) is the third of Robert and Pauline's four children. He pressed his father to write down his memories, and since Robert's death he has followed that path in other ways. With Pauline, he researched and co-edited this book, which grew from involvement in a scholarly edition of the Greek text published in Athens in 2018.[1] His reflections close the book as Part VI.

Other people have played important roles in the gradual evolution of this book, and we are grateful for the contribution of each one. Professor Fragiski Ampatzopoulou, who edited the new Greek edition, provided the impetus to gather memories and material. Dimitrios Varvaritis generously shared his research into Isaac Matarasso's publications and unpublished reports, providing an invaluable inventory that helped clarify key points in the story. Eleni Beze, a historian and herself the granddaughter of the printer and fellow survivor who published . . . *And Yet Not All Died* . . . in 1948, provided precious information about IM's post-war work for the Jewish communities of Salonica and Greece. Rena Molho has offered knowledge and support over many years. Thanks are also due to Dom Erik Varden OCSO and

Dr Brian Klug, Senior Tutor in philosophy at St Benet's Hall, Oxford. The events described here have touched three generations of the Matarasso family. We remember Albert and Lucie, David, Alice and Haïm; Maurice and Denise, Ninon, Henri, Sam, Nelly, and Charlie; and thank the younger members: Paul; Martine, Michel; Aliki, Nora; and Isaac's other grandchildren, Pascale, Antoine, and Veronique.

This book places all the writings of Isaac Matarasso on the Shoah in Salonica before English-speaking readers for the first time.[2] It has allowed the family to provide a proper context, in which personal memory, letters and other documents all play a part. It will be evident from the book's diverse voices, as well as its uncertainties and gaps, that this account makes no claim of finality. But it is closed, as far as the family is concerned: a sacred duty imposed by the custodianship of those primary sources is being discharged. What is known is made available here, and historians can draw on these sources in the continuing task of understanding what happened in Salonica, in Greece and in Europe during the Nazi period. Memory that does not become history is lost. This book is an attempt to ensure that what must not be lost is remembered. It is, after all, necessary to say it again.

I

An urgent conversation

Pauline Matarasso

'Je lis trois fois vos lettres. Lisez deux fois les miennes.'[*]

BEARING WITNESS

The tale presented on these pages in book form is layered with meanings. It is first and foremost a story, a true-to-life story – a true-to-death story. The events that make it a story were lived, seen or heard by those who later wrote them down: the witnesses. And in the words of witnesses events live on with a unique authenticity so long as there are others left to say: 'I saw them, touched them, ate with them, and they were men and women you can trust.'

The principal document was written between January 1945 and January 1946 by Isaac Matarasso, my father-in-law.[3] It describes events that took place during and immediately after the German occupation of Salonica – that is, between April 1941 and January 1945 – events the writer saw with his own eyes, or through those of others who were present. It is thus a witness account, not far removed in its immediacy from that of the news reporter, as much of it was written up from notes, jotted down day by day and passed to the press as early as March 1946.[4] The driving motive was his passionate wish that *the world might know.* This urgency can be felt all the way from the Preface, where the dead, the members of his community, come to ask the writer 'Why?' and charge him with their message 'Tell the living', to the Epilogue, where he spells it out:

> We must beware.
> Lightning strikes at random.
> Disasters give no warning.
> Be on your guard.
> We all have a part to play in preventing further cataclysms
> from engulfing mankind.

The Preface and Epilogue bookend a story that can be read as a series of conversations with different interlocutors: with himself, with members of the Jewish Council, with friends in the ghetto, with his torturers, with survivors from the camps, with you and me. He represents his whole community as lost in circular conversation, 'talking themselves silly'. He writes with the urgency of today's youth fighting for the survival of the planet, and it drives him quite rightly to lay a burden on each one of us.

The fulfilment of his wish was complicated by questions of language. Isaac Matarasso wrote this account in French; it was first published in Salonica, the city he was born and lived in, in Greek. It has lacked until now the complete edition in English that it deserves, and which his family, with the backing of Bloomsbury, can now thankfully provide. It comes too with the addition of material from the family archive, including texts by IM not easily accessible and excerpts from the unpublished memoir of his son Robert, often relating the same events, but as experienced by a teenage boy.

The archive of photographs, documents, letters and texts stretches back more than a hundred years, and has been drawn on to recall a time, a place, a people. Three generations have contributed to the resulting book. The principal, my father-in-law, is the Witness: this book is his. He, I suspect, would say that it belongs to the great multitude of those who died, those he invokes in his Preface, and no one will argue with that. For his son, Robert, the same events became an experience that marked his whole life and which he was attempting to interpret at nearly 40 years' distance. For the next generation one of IM's grandchildren speaks in an afterword. My part is to bear witness to the Witness, as the only person still alive who knew him. I have the further privilege of being his translator.

TIME AND PLACE

Salonica, or Thessaloniki, in the Greek guise it has assumed again after long years of forced estrangement, was an important seaport in Graeco-Roman times, a trading crossroads with a Jewish community and, after a visit by St Paul, a Christian one as well. The city's principal street was part of the Via Egnatia, linking Constantinople to Rome, and its port was one of the finest in the Aegean. Salonica passed the centuries between 'then' and 'now' like most well-positioned and hence prosperous cities: as a sitting prey for hungry neighbours, alternately ransacked and protected. A long period of Byzantine rule in the Middle Ages came to an end in the mid-fifteenth century, when the Ottoman Empire established itself as the dominant force in the Near East and the Balkans. Salonica would remain a prized possession of the caliphate until 1912.

Around 1500 the town's Jewish community was swollen by large numbers of Sephardic Jews expelled from Spain by Ferdinand of Aragon and his more devout and less pragmatic wife, Isabella of Castile. The Ottomans welcomed the Jews into the depleted city and the newcomers flourished in wealth and numbers. They kept their own language, which mutated over time into the form known as Judeo-Spanish or Ladino, and remained the community's mother tongue into the twentieth century. The Jews of Salonica did not provide the city with just one stratum of its population: they grew organically, supplying recruits to every echelon, from the stevedores on the docks to the *haute bourgeoisie*. Above all, they were traders, facilitating the movement of all manner of goods from east to west.

THE FRENCH DIMENSION

Isaac's father, Aaron Matarasso (1850–1943), was such a man, a *zafar*, a trader and dealer in currency and objects of value, whose interests stretched widely, north, west and east. Himself a Judeo-Spanish speaker, he had a competence in many languages – he needed them for business. His children – Albert, Isaac, David, Alice, Nelly and Esther – were of the new generation that embraced French, acquired in the secular schools recently established by the Alliance Israélite Universelle, a Paris-based organization that actively disseminated French culture to Jewish communities in the Ottoman Empire, presenting it as the high point of civilization. Among the educated class of this community French became the language of choice, preferred to the traditional Ladino; it was already the accepted language of diplomacy and culture. Isaac, born in 1892, was Aaron's second son. He and his siblings spoke Ladino with their parents but kept diaries in French, and later spoke mainly French in their homes and with each other. After 1912, Greek became the official language throughout Macedonia, but by that generation, born too soon, it was acquired, rather than absorbed.

Isaac, the cleverest of the three sons, was sent to France in 1911 to study medicine at the University of Toulouse. He left, an Ottoman subject of Jewish nationality, as his identity papers put it. The following year, the First Balkan War brought his home city into the kingdom of Greece, and in 1913, during a visit home, he was issued with his first Greek passport. It does not mention his Jewish identity. The ten years he spent in France were defined in retrospect by the watershed of 1914: on one side *la belle époque*, on the other the First World War and its aftermath. In the golden glow of the first he fell in love with France and all he found there: socialism and science, opera and music hall, intellectual ferment and, most enduringly of all, Andrée Rey, the fair-haired, blue-eyed daughter of a farmer and horse dealer in the Gers who was then living with a married brother in Toulouse. He was passionate too about his studies: both general medicine and his chosen specialism of dermatology. In his mind's eye he saw himself settled in France, putting up a brass name plate outside the door, raising a family. On a visit home in August 1914 he observed with dread the outbreak of the war in Europe and wrote to the girl he loved:

> When will we see each other again? October will soon be here . . . oh, if only the war would end . . . and if it doesn't I'll do my utmost to enlist in France as a volunteer.[5]

In the end, he spent part of the war in a horse-drawn vehicle on narrow country roads, replacing more experienced doctors needed for the wounded. At home, Salonica was garrisoned by thousands of French, British and other troops defending the Macedonian front against the Central Powers.

The year 1918 fell like a guillotine across his plans for the future. Albert, his elder brother, had arrived the year before in Lyon, intending to join cousins active in the silk trade. Isaac's mother, Tamar, accompanied by his younger sisters Nelly and Esther, risked the sea journey to visit her sons and report back on their new ventures. A studio photograph records the happy visit to the medical student in Toulouse, Isaac standing confidently behind his seated mother, the girls beside them, one perched on a stool, already *la jeune fille*, the younger still quite a child. It was the last trace they would leave: on 13 January 1918, as mother and daughters returned to Salonica, a prowling submarine torpedoed their ship off the coast of Sardinia.[6] All three were drowned; Aaron lost nearly half his family.

Over the next two years it became clear to Isaac that filial duty called him home. Clear too is what it cost him. Among his few papers he kept an eloquent testimonial from the Syndicat des Pêcheurs de Marseille addressed to persons unknown, pleading for this particular young doctor to be appointed to the outlying quarter of l'Estaque, where he had made himself indispensable during a recent epidemic:

In the name of our syndicated fishermen we declare that Dr Isaac Matarasso has employed his medical skills to great effect in serving the inhabitants of the district of l'Estaque. His services were particularly appreciated during the influenza epidemic which swept through our neighbourhood during 1918. It is our urgent wish and request that Dr Matarasso be reappointed here.

How many lives need to be touched to coalesce into an official appeal of this kind? But he had given his word, and some time in 1920, the year when the fishermen's request was made, he embarked for home.

RETURN TO SALONICA

His fiancée, Andrée, followed him to Salonica. How and when Isaac prepared his father to receive a French Catholic daughter-in-law I never thought to ask; but according to Sam Benrubi, Isaac's nephew and, during his last illness, confidant, the news did not initially go down well. If the Matarassos were an easy-going clan, who kept religious festivals more as family occasions than solemn holy days, the community was nonetheless protective of its identity. Marrying out was very rare. Isaac was the son for whom most had been done and of whom most was probably expected. He in turn was prepared to give much, but not to give way in this. He held his own, and it was, as it usually is, the father who gave in, with good grace and no cause for subsequent regret.

What Andrée thought she kept to herself – the habit of a lifetime – but what she did is eloquent enough. She followed the man she loved to a far country, where everything would be strange and her in-laws might not like her. On her arrival, the couple were married according to the Jewish rite. That there was no alternative is immaterial, the young woman's resolve to embrace her husband's culture being without reserve. She even learned Ladino, though never more than a smattering of Greek.

In a postcard to a Salonican friend settled in France, dated 25 June 1921, Isaac depicts with humour a holiday idyll he and Andrée were then enjoying:

The spot I am in with Andrée is glorious [. . .] We walk through the fields picking flowers and are installed, French middle-class style, in a hotel where the facilities are what are termed modern. I love it here and, were there no Salonica, I'd have turned shepherd. Andrée would be Chloë.

But there *was* Salonica, and both he and the city had changed during his years away. Whereas the man stood poised now to fulfil his earlier promise, the city had undergone a chaotic transfer of rule from Istanbul to Athens, a traumatic exchange of populations and, in 1917, a devastating fire that destroyed two-thirds of the built-up area and occasioned large-scale emigration, notably of the Jewish population. The man had advanced; the city, at least temporarily, had regressed. A letter from 1921, to the same friend in France, gives the depth of his disappointment:

Heat, mosquitoes, the drachma falling through the floor, obligatory conscription for Jews, despair and in its wake venereal diseases, gains to be made in the drachma, less so as regards the rest [. . .]

Well, my dear Vidal, what really matters is not to be found in Salonica. Neither satisfaction, nor monetary advantage, nor esteem compensate for the intellectual life that one can't enjoy here.

Next year I might come and spend a few weeks with you.

Andrée sends greetings. My kind regards to your wife and to your parents.

Your Old Chap[7]

PROFESSIONAL AND FAMILY LIFE

The birth of a long-awaited child in 1927 anchored the couple. The extended family group was close in every way. On the other side of Tsimiski Street lived Aaron Matarasso with his remaining daughter, Alice, married to Haïm Benrubi. Since the tragedy of 1918 Aaron had retired from business, applying his time and resources to a charity that provided support to the poorest in the Jewish community. After his death, in 1943, he would be remembered as 'A modest and good man, much of whose life was given over to the public good, without ostentation or vainglory'.[8] The child cousins were in and out of each other's homes. Summer holidays were taken in Slovenia, together with David's family. By the 1930s there was no more talk of France, and only one occasion when Isaac Matarasso took his wife and son back to visit her family on the farm in the Gers. Perhaps the gulf had grown too wide to bridge. Yet in some secret place Andrée's French identity lay stowed. It surfaced in sentences starting *'Nous autres Français. . .'* that heralded a point to be made, a lesson on how something should – or more probably should not – be done. The dutiful daughter-in-law also began attending Mass at the Lazarist church on Christian feast days, together with her circumcised son when he grew old enough. Her in-laws were unbothered, while between husband and wife the mutual tolerance and respect in matters of religion never wavered; if anything, it grew.

Family and professional life went hand in hand in the 1920s and '30s, the period when Isaac Matarasso established his reputation as a dermatologist. His career suffered indubitably from the return to Salonica. It was hard for the young man, without contact with his peers or access to the latest facilities provided by laboratories, to carve out for himself a position at the cutting edge of research. Yet working on his own, in a relative backwater, and without collaboration or resources, he developed a treatment for the permanent removal of freckles, which was simple, cheap, safe, virtually painless and 100 per cent effective. Freckles run the gamut from quite attractive to gravely disfiguring. Cases of the latter were not rare among Sephardic Jews and, in the culture of the time, risked blighting a girl's marriage prospects. Dr Matarasso, being well supplied with them himself, stood in for the patient in his own experiments. His method consisted in fabricating, in the simplest possible way, pencils of carbon dioxide in the form of dry ice, which were applied to individual freckles for a calibrated number of seconds. The whole procedure from start to finish could take place *in situ*; the only cost involved was the physician's time, the number of treatments being proportionate to the extent of the disfigurement. His lucid – and illustrated – exposition of his work was published in 1932 in the *Annales de Dermatologie*, where it attracted interest and respect. One Paris dermatologist, when consulted by wealthy Jews from Salonica, would send them home, saying: 'Where do you come from? Oh [. . .] You'd do better to consult Dr Matarasso, his knowledge is greater than mine.'

Most dermatologists also practised as venereologists: the two specialisms traditionally go together, and this was the case from the outset with Isaac Matarasso. Besides his ground-breaking work on the elimination of freckles, he published at least six other articles in a French medical journal between 1922 and 1938.[9] Here was an experimental scientist steadily at work, hampered only by the limited facilities at his disposition, and who, had he settled in

France, would have gone far in his chosen profession. Nonetheless, it was the healer in him who gave direction to Isaac's life, and that healer was no respecter of either diseases or persons. '*Je suis docteur*' was the response given to an attempt by Elizabeth Arden to entice him to Paris to work on her beauty products. It was as a general practitioner that he 'held twice weekly a free evening surgery in one of the poorest districts of the town', to which his small son, Robert, would sometimes accompany him.[10] Not only were these consultations free; often the remedies were free too, whether made up by himself or taking the form of samples left by travelling salesmen. He held to these habits throughout the Occupation, when acting as part of a team treating the sick and injured on their return from forced labour or when visiting the poor in the ghetto, although there he characteristically gives the credit to his colleague Dr Amariglio: 'Joseph spent more time with the poor. He knew how to talk to them, he was used to it.'[11] Modesty, but also the light, ironic touch, as though he was not 'used to it' himself.

His family sometimes thought he overdid the altruism in his last years of failing health, when his earnings were barely enough to live on, but he would have none of it: 'I want to take an interest in all that needs setting to rights round about [. . .] and one can't mend anything except by giving a personal example of integrity, kindness and the gift of self', he wrote to me in 1956.[12] His needs, like his income, had always been moderate. His leisure occupations were swimming, hill-walking and sitting with friends on café terraces watching the world go by. He never had a car; his most precious possession – later surrendered to the Germans – was a large radio he could tune into broadcasts from all over Europe. After the war, in Athens, he gave his consultations in a room in the family flat, with the entrance hall doubling as a waiting room: a man of high intelligence, simple tastes and no pretensions.

On the surface, the 1930s presented few problems for the wider Matarasso family: life was good. The only outward change was the departure in 1937 of the Benrubis to Athens and the patriarch's move to a residential home a few minutes' walk away. Yet no one could live through those years without a growing sense of foreboding. In Isaac Matarasso's case this was balanced by a deep-seated desire to find the good in the world, above all in people. Optimism is too facile a word. *Espérance* – theological hope – comes closest, although he would not have used it; but one can know the meaning of a word one has never met with, live out a concept one could not define. His habitual vocabulary was that of the liberal philosophy popular in late nineteenth-century France, and his knowledge of Hebrew was probably limited to the prayers of the great occasions, unlike that of his friend Joseph Amariglio, who both read and commented on the Bible in Hebrew.[13] Yet his reading of Jewish writers was, I believe, wider than his entourage suspected. A letter shows him quoting with familiarity Maimonides, not merely an authority on the Torah but a philosopher and theologian who embraced both Aristotle and the Neo-Platonists, influencing in turn Catholic theologians across the wide spectrum from Aquinas to Eckhardt:

As for the tensions between generations, they are as common as those among the old, or the young. To criticize is open to all – it can be a weakness or a strength. In the service of a just and rational mind it is man's greatest asset. No hatred, ever. I think I told you what Maimonides said: 'To criticize is not an offence, on the contrary heaven rewards it. I prize it as being a divine calling.'

These words were written to his son in 1955, and he was surely harking back to older conversations, but his nephew, Sam Benrubi, remembered Isaac always with a book in his hands, even in his last years. Whenever there was no specific call on his time, he said, he would pick up a book. My own impression is that IM's interest lay more in ideas than fiction, and this is confirmed by dedications in the rare volumes that we know to have passed through his hands. The first is a copy of Joseph Nehama's classic *Histoire des Israélites de Salonique*, published in 1935 and inscribed by the author to *'l'ami et le frère intellectuel dont j'aime la droiture, la bonté foncière et la largeur de vues. En toute affection.'** These qualities, recognized by one outstanding man in another, are evident in his life, but it is the breadth of mind that I should like to comment on briefly here. This Jew, rooted in his own culture, none the less wore no blinkers, and even in the aftermath of a world torn apart sought only unity. He came out of hell with his beliefs not destroyed, not even damaged, but whole, and – I would venture – enhanced. Another dedication, this time of his own book to a colleague, shows the very qualities mentioned by Nehama:

---

* 'To my friend and my brother in thought, in whom I love the depth of goodness and the breadth of understanding, with all my heart, Joseph Nehama.'

Il fallait du courage pour s'opposer à l'action criminelle des Nazis pendant l'occupation. Il fallait beaucoup de bonté et un grand esprit Chrétien pour abriter et protéger des Israélites Héllènes poursuivis à mort par les SD. Le Docteur Milt. Gaïtanakis a eu cette bonté et ce courage. Je lui adresse mon admiration reconnaissante.*

And in the letter to us written in 1955, praising Maimonides, he broadens his embrace still further:

It is the first day of Rosh Hashanah (the start of the New Year). According to the Bible we are in the year 5,716. Does that mean that 3,861 years before the Christian era we had recognized that God was One? Perhaps. And that this God manifested himself to mankind 1955 years ago? Surely. And since then humanity has been ever striving to improve.

WITNESSING: SELF-PERCEPTION AND THE SHARING OF ROLES

Greece's involvement in the Second World War began on 28 October 1940 with the irruption of a predatory Italian force across the Albanian border. After fierce fighting in harsh winter conditions, a Greek army, which included 13,000 Jewish soldiers, drove them back. Italian failure brought a swift reaction. On 6 April 1941 Germany invaded

---

* 'It took courage to stand up to the criminal actions of the Nazis during the occupation. It took real goodness and a great Christian spirit to shelter and protect Greek Jews hunted to death by the SD. Dr Milt[iades] Gaïtanakis had this goodness and this courage. I offer him my grateful admiration.' [SD: Sicherheitsdienst, the intelligence agency of the SS.]

in force, sweeping east and south and chasing out as they went a British Expeditionary Force of 60,000. On 9 April the Wehrmacht rolled into Salonica. Content to leave the Peloponnese to the Italians, they spread across Macedonia, quartering themselves in its principal city. The Jewish community looked on with dread.

Isaac Matarasso's narrative covers the three and a half years of the German occupation. The first thing that needs saying is that it is not about *him*. It is not *his* war. He observed and wrote as a man of science, at a time when science held the key to the secrets of the universe and the hope of progress, so he never lost sight of the horizon. He was also a member of a community with particularly clear contours in both time and space, and he wrote very consciously in the name of that community and in the names of its dead. He writes as their representative, therefore his own journey is irrelevant. In the Preface he distances himself by using the 'we' of the nineteenth-century French historian, which produces the unlikely but charming 'we let a milestone take our weight'. At specific moments in the account, where he is clearly an eyewitness, he still writes 'we', sometimes for the same reason, sometimes because he was indeed not alone but one of a small team of doctors called in at a time of crisis, to work at the station, in a synagogue or doing home visits.

When the 'I' suddenly appears, it calls us to a different kind of attention, for what then follows are his reflections and not the echo of a common experience. Thus we listen to him on the members of the Community Council, and note that his comments are both urgent and subtle, measured and hesitant to condemn:

I see them still, those men, intelligent, honest, but credulous and faint-hearted, acting with the meek eagerness of the servile accustomed to passive obedience, unquestioning and utterly uncritical, and who strive to anticipate orders so as to carry them out before they are put into words. These men erupt into the administrative offices, demanding records, issuing orders, correcting a list of figures here or there, above all berating any employee seen to be a trifle slow: 'God Almighty! Where's your sense of urgency?' For it was a matter of urgency to satisfy the Chief Rabbi, who in turn must satisfy the Germans who needed (we found this out later) to supply their gas chambers and crematoria. Oh what a hideous tragi-comedy!

He was, he says, a witness, '*un témoin*'. He does not claim to have seen it all with his own eyes. He was not a news reporter looking on but a member of a suffering community, and he criticizes the Chief Rabbi, Zvi Koretz, in whom he has little or no confidence, in the name of that community. Throughout he remains what he always was: a combination of scientist and healer. The scientist observes with a degree of detachment; the healer, to a different degree, identifies with the patient. This 'double vision', with the observer looking through one eye and the physician through the other, is apparent in the very first account of mass brutality inflicted on the Jewish population, when, on 11 July 1942, 9,000 Jewish men were lined up in Eleftherias Square, made to stand for hours in the scorching sun, beaten and eventually conscripted as slave labourers.[14] An eyewitness account, no doubt. Well, no, as it happens – or not directly his. Thirty-eight years later his son widened the context for us. Giving first a résumé of the same events, with his father's version before him (some of the phrases used are identical), he rotates the picture, not without appreciating the effect thus obtained:

> Mr Barzilaï paused, choking on the words as he described the ordeal of so many of his friends that he had witnessed from his windows overlooking the square. He had run breathless and grey to our house bearing the news. Both my father and I were outside the prescribed age and had stayed at home that day. My father had closed the shutters, ostensibly to keep the sun out, and in the semi-darkness of the room, was sitting very silent. Barzilaï, unable to utter another word, was shaking so badly that [our maid] brought him a glass of cool rose water, and with a trace of affectionate familiarity, whispered gently to him: 'Drink it, Mr Barzilaï, drink it, please . . ..' He drank the scented liquid and gradually regained some of his calm.
>
> 'We must do something, Isaac', he said sombrely. My father looked up and slowly opened his hands, palms upwards, in a gesture of resigned impotence, and said nothing. They sat there, looking at each other, two old friends whose memories reached back to their childhood and whose grief needed no words, only the silent and almost palpable healing quality of each other's presence. I felt excluded, an intruder in this silent dialogue.[15]

No longer one witness but three, all silent now: one to see, one to write and one to bring the two to life, giving the episode a striking depth of focus. The first two are essential and are validated by the third.

FRAGMENTATION

The last 18 months of the war are those in which least is known about Isaac Matarasso's life, in so far as it differed, that is, from the lives of the majority of his community. And clearly it did differ, in that at the Liberation he was still alive, and thus no longer representative of a community in whose name he could say 'we'. Writing later of this interval between the deportations of March–August 1943 and the departure of the Germans in October 1944, he touches on the hidden – and dangerous – lives of those who escaped in ones and twos, giving most space, as of right, to a handful recaptured and left in Salonican prisons, where fate seemed to have spared them, only to be shot at the last. He himself is absent from these pages, as he was in reality, and has to rely here on the witness of others.

He is a witness again when the first survivors trickle back from Poland in the early weeks of 1945. He too is once again in Salonica, but these few are now the true witnesses and he is their recorder, pen in hand: 'we listened, we heard what they said, we learned to believe the unbelievable'. He spends many days examining, in his professional capacity, those who have suffered experiments at the hands of other doctors who disgraced their calling. His too was a hands-on experience, horrifying and moving – but of course he does not say so, he writes a report. He dates and signs it. The historian's 'we' appears again for the last time in the epilogue, but here it embraces you, me, all of us.

TIGHTENING THE NOOSE

We might think it appropriate to follow his example and leave him in his chosen role, as the man who stands aside and speaks for those who have suffered and died. Certainly he made a conscious effort to maintain his role as witness: in the hundred or so pages of his account he mentions his son once, his wife not at all. To place in the public domain the life of someone one has known and loved – not least for their reticence – is a delicate decision. Yet to leave things unsaid and truth unspoken can open the door to misunderstandings, and it seems right to draw on such unpublished sources as his family has to hand. Robert, 14 years old at the beginning of the Occupation, started writing down, in the two or three years before his death in 1982, what he remembered of that time. Bearing the scars of an experience undergone at such a vulnerable age, he was exploring his own self-understanding, so his is an 'I' narrative, rather than a 'we' or a 'they'. The focus and angle are different, and often supply information missing from his father's account. Regrettably, the memoir is left suspended in mid-March 1943. We read of the first train leaving 'for Kraków', turn the page and find lists of words, handwritten, cryptic, devoid of syntax. Having stared long at this coded information, I think I have made sense of most of it. Some of it I have known since 1949, when I heard it directly from Robert, and what I heard then stands corroborated by what he wrote later. It is a story I shall now attempt to tell, knitted together from these disparate materials.

The summer of 1942 had brought to Salonica Dr Max Merten, a lawyer charged with the city's military administration, who would collaborate fully with the Gestapo in the destruction of the Jewish community. We have glimpsed already the first restrictions and the introduction of forced labour. By the beginning of February 1943, when Adolf Eichmann's 'experts' Dieter Wisliceny and Alois Brunner, who had already proved themselves elsewhere, arrived to take charge of the deportation programme, the browbeaten community was approaching a state of psychological and moral paralysis. This left the Germans free to tighten their grip with a series of edicts and orders, restricting freedom of movement and communication, announcing the creation of a ghetto and the implementation on 6 February 1943 of the Nuremberg race laws. The hidden purpose was the deportation to Auschwitz in a matter of weeks of the entire community.

The first official news of these measures was brought to the Matarasso family by a neighbour employed in the Town Hall. It was baleful. The race laws were already familiar from their application in Germany and the occupied territories. It is not my impression that IM ever thought his wife's Catholicism would shield himself and their son from their implementation: he presents the order as posted up by the occupying authority with its various clauses clearly listed. Hope, of course, is hard to stifle utterly. Robert records a visit the previous summer from the priest at the Lazarist Mission – Monsignor Katz, a Dutchman with fluent French, who knew the family well. Robert came in to find documents lying on the table, certificates brought by the priest, who had been at pains to procure them, where necessary, from France. The only surviving document is dated 3 February 1943. It is a certificate on the headed paper of the Mission attesting that Andrée Matarasso had been duly baptized, was and remained a practising Roman Catholic. It gives her date and place of birth and the names of her parents. Her son is nowhere mentioned. It is signed by Father Katz, whose signature has been validated on the reverse by the Archbishop of Athens and the French Consul. They countersigned it on 15 March, when the family were already in the ghetto.

THREE WEEKS IN THE GHETTO

The orders published on 6 February announcing the creation of the ghetto, the obligation on all Jews to take up residence by 25 February, the obligatory display on clothes and houses of the Star of David and the implementation of the race laws, left little room for hope. Before 25 February, Andrée packs for the family and the parents walk off to the ghetto, public transport being forbidden them. Robert is sent out on various pretexts and makes his solitary way to join them that evening in the crowded house of his father's colleague Joseph Amariglio, of whom IM would later write a moving portrait. Five rooms in the house, sheltering 28 people in all: the cooking and washing arrangements must have strained the women's resources to the utmost.

The ghetto was closed on 6 March 1943. Around this time there was a little spate of escapes, mostly by young men unburdened with responsibilities, although Isaac's brother David managed to slip away with his wife and two teenage children, shortly after spending 36 hours in the infamous cellars of the Sicherheitsdienst at 42 Velissariou Street. Rumours of all kinds were rife; most were false, but an unexpected easing of the law governing mixed marriages proved to be true. First it was learned in the ghetto that three Jews married to German Aryans had been exempted from wearing the yellow badge and from confinement in the ghetto. A few days later this mitigation was extended to other Jews married to Aryan women – 16 couples in all.

Here, hope glimmered like the half-light of a winter dawn. What could go wrong? Almost anything. Was their documentation sufficient? Would the papers Father Katz had brought to Andrée six months earlier do the trick? Had the time come to play a unique card – let's call it the Joker?

Over the next two or three days events took sudden and unforeseen turns, which yet, with hindsight, seem prepared if not predetermined. Robert's account is rich in detail, and as he was an eye-witness throughout, it will be found in full below.[16] I summarize part of it here because it is essential to the story and raises points that invite discussion.

On 14 March Isaac Matarasso paid a strange visit; he took his son with him, which made it even stranger. Not far from Sarantaporou Street, where they were staying, and almost in the shadow of 42 Velissariou Street, lived a curious couple. RM calls him 'Vladimir Walberg' and his wife 'Poppi'. Walberg was a Jew, a refugee from Russia in the days of Lenin, while his Greek wife was a former dancer at the city's only, and notorious, nightclub. She was much seen with German officers and was now flaunting her acquaintance with Merten, the man with responsibility for 'cleansing' the city of its Jewish population. This relationship had just paid a large dividend in the form of a document from the Kommandantur exempting the Walbergs from all restrictions, and they were on the point of leaving the ghetto. It was to this couple that IM introduced his son. Poppi welcomed 'the Doctor' with almost embarrassing courtesy, and they embarked on a low-toned conversation over coffee, which Robert made a point of not overhearing. Finally his father stood up smiling as Poppi pronounced: 'For you, Doctor, I would do anything, you know that [. . .] Yes, I will speak to Max. I will speak to him tonight. He won't mind since it is the law now [. . .] and anyway, Max will not refuse me anything, you know.'

This curious scene needs decoding. How did these two people, doctor and high-class prostitute, whose lives had apparently nothing in common, know each other, why did

Poppi feel she owed him a favour and why did he take his adolescent son into this louche environment? Last things first: he may have taken his son in part to set a tone, but more significantly he took him because it was *his* life that was at stake, he was the tribute demanded by the monster, in him innocent life silently pleaded for its future. 'Is this your boy, Doctor? What a good-looking lad . . .' Maybe she had no children herself.

Poppi Walberg, it is clear, knew him as a doctor – her doctor, would be an informed guess. If Poppi Walberg went to Dr Isaac Matarasso for treatment for a venereal disease, she would have met with respect, discretion and kindness, by no means guaranteed to prostitutes by the medical profession of that day. What will have troubled him in this exchange of favours was the fact that he was dealing with a collaborator. His rare expressions of contempt are always for Jews who worked for the Germans, who betrayed their co-religionists. Poppi was not a Jew, but her husband was. IM will have felt deeply uncomfortable about approaching her and, via her, the loathed Merten. Yet no one suffered harm, and what he asked for was, as Poppi said, 'the law now'. There have been other descents into the underworld to cheat it of its prey: ultimately he would have thought honour well lost if it bought his son's life, and no moral theologian would disagree. It remains a strange, and strangely human, episode in inhumane times, and one, which, I am sure, was never spoken of afterwards by those involved.

The *Ausweis*, the document that would allow them to live in relative safety outside the confines of the ghetto, had to be fetched from the Kommandantur, itself out of bounds. Joseph Amariglio, friend of many years and never more so than in this time of greatest need, suggested enlisting the invaluable Father Katz once again. The priest turned up the next afternoon. RM remembers:

> He was still with us when we heard the first rumours of the deportation that had taken place early that morning in the suburb of Baron Hirsch. And when, like a blow falling on a bruise, came the news that the sick, the old and the orphans had also been taken away, I instantly knew what this meant, although no one had mentioned my grandfather by name.

Elsewhere Robert gives unique details of that first deportation, and this account has been accepted by Greek historians as authentic.[17] In consequence it has its place here:

> One more event took place that morning in the suburb of Baron Hirsch. A few minutes before the train departed, a convoy of closed lorries was seen approaching the embarkation area. It disgorged a pitiful section of humanity, sick and mentally disturbed people, some of whom had to be carried on stretchers, old men and women and finally 72 young children huddled together, sobbing as only terrified children can. They were the patients of the general and psychiatric hospitals, the inmates of the old people's homes and the children of the orphanage. This small section of the Jewish population had been allowed to remain outside the ghetto, albeit guarded and confined to quarters. Their reprieve had been short-lived. Somewhere in this crowd my grandfather stood alone, because his wife and two daughters had already been killed by the same men but in another war.

These doubly unfortunate people, the young and the old and the suffering, were thus among the first to be deported, on 15 March 1943, and those that survived the horrendous journey will have been murdered on arrival. It was on that same day, according to RM's account, that the family learned of the deportation of the 90-year-old patriarch and of a possible escape for them from the same fate – a hideous contradiction. IM withdrew into silence, to his son's relief. Four decades later, Robert stopped writing at that point in his story, though the reason is uncertain. The last words in his narrative are these:

> I gave him Father Katz's message [that he would be back tomorrow]. He did not reply immediately, then, as if he was trying to reassure me, he said: 'Tomorrow may bring good news . . . .' But of my grandfather, to my relief, he said nothing.

A Gap in the Story

It seems that the invaluable Father Katz did reappear the next day to escort IM to the Kommandantur to fetch the *Ausweis*, and that father, mother and son walked out to a precarious freedom of which we know little. A German Foreign Office document, dated 31 May 1943, reports that in the middle of that month there remained only about 950 Greek Jews in the ghetto, and about 850 Jews of other nationalities living elsewhere in the city: extraordinarily, listed among them is the 'physician Matarasso'.[18] After that, there is no official trace until 1945. The *Ausweis* which saved them from the almost certain death of deportation gave them no protection against death by other means. Within weeks, according to RM's scribbled notes, father and son were arrested by Jewish police – there is some indication of their being betrayed by former friends – and taken back into the ghetto, to Velissariou Street, for interrogation. Isaac alone is qualified to speak of that experience, and has done so: his account is below. The two of them were later moved to Heptapyrgion Prison and kept apart. Time passed. Days, weeks, months, Robert lost count. In fact it was in June that IM was approached by a guard and told that the *andartes* (guerrilla resistance forces) were in need of a doctor. He refused to go unless his son went with him. A second message brought agreement to this, and they were in due course smuggled out, taken to a safe house and from there into the mountains, where they were delivered to a band of men led by a certain Vardas. Parted again from his father, the son, viewed no doubt as a bit of a liability, was hived off to another group, where he did his best to make himself useful. There followed 16 months of hard and dangerous living and, for a boy, grim moments, before father, mother and son were reunited in a liberated Salonica, where nothing was left of their past except the most important – Andrée had been taken in by a Swiss Jewish couple (the husband, I believe, was the acting Swiss Consul) and had spent the last 18 months with them under diplomatic protection.

The Aftermath

On his return from a perilous existence, practising medicine at the most basic level in a harsh environment while being tracked by German troops who burned villages – women and children included – in reprisal for the activities of the partisans, IM dedicated himself to healing the wounds of his community. In early November 1944, a few days after the German withdrawal, a first meeting of survivors was held in the Monasteriote Synagogue, which had survived because of its use by the Red Cross as a store. Isaac Matarasso was elected to take charge of organizing medical services for the surviving community, an event he notes in his book without mentioning his own part in the work.[19] It was a huge responsibility. People surfaced in ones and twos – few families were intact – from hiding, from the hills and countryside, eventually from the camps, to a city in utter chaos. They had only what they stood up in. No doubt he didn't have much more himself, but fortunately a doctor can practise his profession almost without props; his head, hands, feet and a black bag are all he requires for visiting the sick, and in relieving need he becomes an agent in creating networks and restoring social order.

The task was immense. As he records in the last sections of his book, most people had nowhere to live and no means of earning an income. Famine and destitution were the norm in that winter, made worse by sickness and trauma. In addition, the rights to assistance of different groups were contested. Some were seen as having won more favourable treatment through co-operation with the occupier, including those who returned from Bergen-Belsen. Others, including Resistance fighters, were condemned for leftist politics. The doctor refused to recognize such distinctions, arguing for a humanitarian standard that treated each according to their needs, not their past. At a time of civil war he exposed himself to danger by visiting wounded partisans and defending the right of all community members to the scant medical and financial support the community could provide.[20]

While he struggled, in the months after the Liberation, to heal and support, to negotiate and maintain principles and to help rebuild shattered institutional structures, IM never lost sight of his role as witness to the survivors of the once flourishing community. He observed and recorded as he went about the exhausting daily effort of keeping people alive. There was also the work of organizing his material: questioning, listening, expanding his notes and adding the information gathered from survivors. By the spring of 1946 this work was being published in a new leftist Jewish newspaper, *Israelitikon Vima*, beginning a process of talking about the catastrophic events of the past five years. It would prove extraordinarily slow and long.

He describes survivors as 'among the war's true victims' in their utter destitution. In Paris in the 1950s there were seats in the metro marked '*mutilés de guerre*', reserved for those who had lost a limb, along with the gassed and the blinded, not in the Second World War but in the First. The shell-shocked were not catered for: the authorities assumed they had recovered, now that all was quiet on the western front. IM's post-war pages explore some of these hidden wounds – principally the loss of financial means, homes, employment, means of earning a living, and, worst of all, the disappearance of family members. Yet even he, a doctor, does not give much attention to what is now known as Post-Traumatic Stress Disorder (PTSD), the wounding of the psyche. No doubt he recognized it, as Leon Batis, the first survivor to return from Auschwitz, saw it in himself:

> Perhaps I *am* a bit unhinged. And perhaps too – and this comforts me, if that doesn't sound too cynical – others who come through it, like me, will be unhinged as well!

But the vocabulary did not yet exist, and without the words that define it, the real is strangely hard to recognize. It is in the Preface that IM gives voice to his pain, what is now termed survivor's guilt, the pain of suffering unshared. This piece enables him to distance himself from the personal and to convey the suppressed emotions of survivors. It issues from the hours spent listening to those returning from the camps. If it weeps with the dead, it cries out more urgently to the still unborn. We hear this voice again in the Epilogue and in the unpublished 'Memories from the Ghetto'; it surfaces even in personal letters.

I wonder, nonetheless, how clearly IM saw it nearer home, in his own family, perhaps in himself. They too were survivors, not of Auschwitz but of prison and torture and the prospect of imminent death. They had stood in the presence of evil, which one does not endure unmarked, and many in that situation took refuge once the storm had passed in the nearest place of safety, the one called Silence. It filled up quickly after the war with their friends and relations, who had been on similar journeys. In the outer world few people knew that this place existed; it was well camouflaged and the door was always shut. I, who spent many hours with survivors of both generations, never heard that silence broken, nor did it ever occur to me to break it, partly because I was young and ignorant but also, I think, because it had a certain quality about it – it was at once imperceptible and impermeable. Among the generation who were teenagers during the Occupation and escaped deportation by being always just one step ahead of betrayal to the death squads, the silence kept for 50 years tended to break down in old age. This, I think, is not unusual. The old feel a need to clear the suffocating undergrowth, to breathe freely for the first and last time.

It is my belief that Isaac never retreated into that suffocating silence. His role of witness prevented him – perhaps, in a way, protected him. He *had* to go on listening, questioning, focusing on the task to hand, and November 1955 found him adding handwritten notes to his original typescript.

Good news! A young woman subjected to radiation and a surgical procedure in Auschwitz is pregnant – in her seventh month!

Both describing the evil and helping to repair the consequences demanded, and were given, the full engagement of the man. He was saved too by his love of life. Looking back over many more years than he enjoyed, I can say that I have known no one with a more intense love of life. I think he venerated it. And just as he wrote so that all the world might *know*, I am sure that, had I questioned him, he would have shared with me the saving knowledge – to stop it ever happening again.

Signs of New Growth

In April 1946 the family left for Athens, part of an exodus of Jews from a city that was too empty, too silent, too crowded by ghosts and memories. Other survivors went to Palestine, France or America; the Matarassos chose Athens, where the Benrubis, now their only relatives in Greece, pressed them to come. It was a significant choice, a commitment on the part of both parents to Greece as their home. Isaac joined the Central Council of Jewish Communities in Greece, where he worked for the poor, the sick and the homeless. As civil war gripped the country, he continued, at real risk to himself, to assist Jews who were persecuted for their membership of the Communist Resistance during the German occupation.[21] And he continued, of course, to act as personal physician to many of the survivors that he had first treated in Salonica. In 1948 he published the various articles and reports he had written in a slim volume entitled ... *And Yet Not All Died* ... It was printed by Armando Bezes – like Isaac, a Salonican Jew married to a Christian woman, who had spent part of the war with the Resistance. The publication of the book must have seemed to them a shared effort to make their fellow Greeks understand what had happened. But in the midst of a civil war few had time to think about the last one.

Robert, who had missed his last years at school, was helped back into learning by Brother Athanase of the Frères des Écoles Chrétiennes, and sat the first part of his *baccalauréat* in June 1946 at a special session held in Athens. In the same year he was issued with a certificate from the re-established Jewish Community to the effect that, although born of an Aryan mother, he had been subjected to the race laws, confined in the ghetto and then forced into hiding. There is no mention of time spent with the *andartes*, and for good reason. The Communist-led ELAS, responsible for extracting the Matarassos from prison, spent most of 1946–49 in armed struggle with the government. Robert, seen with a Communist newspaper in the street, was picked up by the police. He got away with a beating that left a lump on his head that, in his children's eyes, rivalled in glory the bent German bullet that had narrowly missed him a year earlier.

Death had been close to both father and son during the Occupation, and for Andrée, living in constant fear for the two of them, it may well have been worse. All three had seen too much, heard too much, endured too much, while knowing that they were among the fortunate. Unsurprisingly, each seems to have been led to explore the inner landscape of belief. It may well be that before the war religion had played a minor, even negligible, part in their lives. Those of the next generation who have spoken of their parents' faith have been, in general, dismissive: David had no time for religion; Isaac practised a scientific detachment; Andrée had embraced the cultural practices of her in-laws. To some degree we see in others what we want to see, and I am no exception. I do not, however, think that anybody with an open mind could read the portraits of Harbi Haïm Habib and Joseph Amariglio and think that IM was anything but moved by and open to the spiritual heritage of his forefathers. It may have been an experience quickened to new life in the ghetto, but it was real. Andrée will have needed and received the support of Father Katz, whom Robert shows as closely involved with the family at the most critical and distressing moments. Robert himself, a cosseted only son, was cruelly exposed to terror, danger, loneliness and much brutality. He took the decision to seek baptism in the spring of 1945, and Brother Athanase stood godfather to his pupil. A more surprising ceremony took place around that time: Father Katz conducted a religious marriage for Isaac and Andrée. My impression is that it was performed privately at home, with no one present but their son, and this seems entirely likely. Both, despite Isaac's outward bonhomie, were deeply private people, and neither would have wished to ruffle, however slightly, the serenity of broader family relationships. My understanding is that Andrée also, in her fears and isolation, had found strength in her religion and was glad when Father Katz offered her the opportunity to regularize her situation. The marriage was in the nature of a thanksgiving – for life and health and safety, for a love that stretched back 30 years and more, faithful, devoted and acknowledging no boundaries. It was, above all, a gift that Isaac could offer to his wife, an unconditional return.

By the time I met them in the spring of 1949 the Matarasso family had made a home in a street of three-storeyed houses with tall windows, each giving on to a balcony. Their second-floor, all-purpose flat had a central living room, its focus the big rectangular table which brought friends and family together, with a bedroom giving off it at either end. The doctor's surgery was on the other side of the hall, and beyond it lay the kitchen, the preserve of Andrée and the maid, from which calls of *'Grigora, grigora!'* ('Quickly, quickly!') heralded the approach of mealtimes. Patients waited in the hall. Isaac Matarasso was 54 years old, his vigour as yet unimpaired. His work potential was still considerable, but building a practice in a new city was going to be hard. In 1949 his son, in his turn, left to study in France and was not expected back, income and outgoings were only just in balance and life had been left hollowed out by the Shoah. And yet the man I saw at rare and precious moments during what proved to be the last years of his life was rich in warmth, enthusiasm and, yes, joy.

THE LAST YEARS

In the winter of 1951–52 Isaac Matarasso came to Paris. Both his brothers were now there: Albert, the elder, manufacturing gas fittings in Suresnes; David, more peripatetic, with business interests in France, Switzerland

and Brazil. The war had taken its tribute from both families and left damage in its wake: in the long term there would be no happy endings. Isaac had come to visit his son, left struggling by a disrupted education: he would have liked to be a doctor like his father, but it wasn't going to happen.

Time spent with us was Isaac's delight. He loved the young:

> What I love in the young is their youth. This sounds stupid, but you might be surprised to know that a lot of the old are indifferent to the beauty of youth. They don't notice the harmonious movements of a young couple, the effortlessness of their gestures, the supple grace of their postures, the quickness of their every movement, in a word that youth which we once had and which they are kind enough to give us another glimpse of.[22]

Quite unaware of these flights, I only knew he was easy for a shy girl to talk to. He never put anyone down – when he declared that I wasn't a workhorse, I inferred from his manner that I must be something better. At that time I was in fact sitting in the Bibliothèque Sainte-Geneviève, preparing a thesis on a twelfth-century *chanson de geste*. My future father-in-law accorded a disproportionate importance to this piece of medieval arcana. It was his baby by proxy; its progress kept his reserve of hope topped up throughout his final illness. There was a long labour, and the final *accouchement* was touchingly applauded three weeks before he died: 'I have built up a large store of joy, satisfaction, pride even. This wasn't just a success, it was a triumph!'[23] He had waited faithfully through six years and two real babies.

As the wedding had been in England, to allow for a brief inspection of Robert by his new English relatives, it had seemed only fair to spend the honeymoon in Athens, submitting myself to Jewish–Greek scrutiny. It was late July and very hot, and a honeymoon shared with one's in-laws in their flat, plus a stream of unknown visitors, is unusual, but their kindness and, above all, the simplicity of their approach were disarming, and, having no expectations, I was very malleable.

We saw them again in Paris sooner than we expected: a health alert had brought Isaac to consult a respected physician. Our then flat consisted of two small rooms and a galley kitchen with a cold tap on the sink. No bathroom. A shared toilet off the staircase. Matter-of-factly they settled in; they had known worse. We two moved around the corner to a hotel that was equally basic. I cannot now remember whether at night we left the puppy with them or took it with us.

Two years later their first grandchild was born in rural Burgundy. Andrée arrived first and cooked a trussed chicken for the christening, having previously, in a conjuring trick I have never attempted to repeat, boned it, and – hey presto! – it became a trussed chicken that one could slice. *Grandpère* followed soon after and pronounced the baby perfect; after that he inspected the rest of the stock: two cows, half a dozen goats, poultry, a workhorse (not me). Desperate to help, he was given a paintbrush and a tin of creosote and weatherproofed a barn door. Wherever he went, he made friends. An elderly neighbour had suffered all her life from a disfiguring allergy to sunlight. He took a prescription to the nearest chemist, had it made up as a *pommade* and effected a miracle cure. Long after he died prescription and *pommade* went on serving their purpose. How I wish I had questioned him when he mentioned in passing that cobwebs (like burned cotton wool) were very effective in stopping bleeding from a wound. Where did he learn that magic formula? Was it Sephardic lore, handed down the centuries in Ladino, or did he hear it first from the peasants in the mountain villages of Macedonia, where pharmaceutical supplies will have varied from unreliable to non-existent? The properties of a spider's web have recently moved from old wives' tale to innovative science, but it appears that Dr Matarasso got there first.

Today I still see the four of us sitting round the table at lunchtime, and Papa trying a mouthful before saying, reflectively, 'Delicious, but it could have done with just a pinch more salt'; whereupon I would protest that Maman had worked in the kitchen all morning and why did he have to criticize? I don't remember him quoting Maimonides on the divine property of criticism, but I never knew him irritated or impatient; Maman meanwhile sat sphinx-like and smiled. That was in 1955, the last time I saw him. Less than two years later we moved to England, another farm, another baby; a dozen letters still survive, and then there is silence.

His letters must have come all through those months and the years before like a fluttering of doves. Why were they not all treasured and kept? Full of gifts and surprises, they are surely among the least self-centred letters ever written by someone terminally ill. What had been prostate cancer now spread into the bones. He referred to it as arthritis, and, as he was the doctor, nobody gainsaid him. To me it seemed a kind of charade: he couldn't *really* believe it, and if he didn't, why was everyone playing this game? No doubt they found it easier, and that was partly a cultural thing, but I think that on his part it corresponded to something deeper. His love of life expressed itself in terms of undying hope, of unquenchable enthusiasm. He had faith in his own body – it had never let him down:

> I have confidence in life, which I love. I have confidence in my own body, far more intelligent than us doctors, and Papa still keeps his courage up, while loving all manner of things, yet coveting none.

A visit from Robert in December 1956 released fresh energy, enough to walk round Athens on glorious sunny days, talking their heads off:

> And almost daily we exchanged views on human reactions, emotional and spiritual, and on the young climbing the hill of life and the old scrambling up behind. It was when our ideas clashed that I gained the most.[24]

A few weeks earlier he had been awarded the Prix Desportes by the Académie Nationale de Médecine in Paris, in recognition of his work on freckles, still considered cutting-edge. In spirit he never gave up seeing patients. When the pain got too bad, he ceased to consult . . . until it abated.

> My career is on the back burner just now. I haven't lost hope of getting back in the traces. If my joints and my general health leave a lot to be desired at present, my brain and my intellectual curiosity are as vigorous as ever. I shall never lose heart, even if I'm on crutches. At present a stout stick is all I need.

He wrote this on the last day of September 1957, but determination in the face of cancer can only go so far. I don't think he actually consulted after that.

There were other pleasures when pain allowed. Opening forgotten drawers in desks, fingering old papers, discovering photographs: salvaged memories acted as a tonic for him. One might have thought the past contained too many horrors to be willingly revisited, but no. Clearly, whatever housekeeping he had done there had somehow sanitized it. The suffering is contained between the covers of his book; the writing has itself been a means of purgation and healing. The pain of his last years was of a different kind, without an admixture of evil. Christmas 1957 even brought a gift of remission:

> The weather today was heavenly. I sat in the sun on the balcony for an hour. I saw passers-by in their Sunday best, I felt the sun, which shines on me too, I looked at the streets which belong to me as well as to everyone else. I saw myself again pain-free and at ease at the seaside, in the hills, elsewhere. It's a long illness, but my body is holding its own. I haven't lost weight this past fortnight, 50 kg at least and good quality at that!

And he wouldn't let pain have the last word:

> They say that those who have suffered much are admitted to heaven. Suffering sanctifies us a little, it purifies us.

He died three weeks later, on 22 January 1958. Andrée outlived him by less than four years. His letters are full of tributes to her care: 'Pray for Maman's health as much as for mine. She is precious to me, she's my doctor.' She moved to a small flat closer to the Benrubis. In 1960, unwell, she went to Paris for tests. I went to fetch her, and she spent some time with us and met two grandchildren Isaac had never known. But England was a step too far, and she was glad to return to the country that had so long been her home. Shortly before she died, Alice Benrubi asked her where she wanted to be buried. Did she want a Catholic funeral? She had spent her life with Isaac, she said, and she wanted to lie beside him now. The kaddish was said over her in the presence of their son. This last exchange of courtesies, where each in turn adopted the liturgical language of the other to express their love, confirmed a passing through the tension of paradox to its resolution in unity. Isaac put into words what both lived in silence:

True religion flourishes in the hearts of all who love their neighbours – animals included.

A Note on the Texts

THE DOCUMENTS

The central texts translated and published here were typed by their author on thin paper. IM took care over the visual appearance of the typescript, spacing, capitalizing and underlining words for emphasis in the days before computers put bold and italic type at everyone's fingertips.

As far as possible, the distinctive character of his text has been preserved: when he capitalizes the names of Nazi criminals and their collaborators, his text resembles an indictment, which he certainly intended it to be. All footnotes, except for occasional translations into English, are by IM and figure in the typescript: endnotes have been prepared by the editors to help contemporary readers. For the same reason, small changes have been made to the sequencing of the final sections so that they reflect historical chronology more clearly.

Two sections of the typescript have been left out of this book for differing reasons. The first instance concerns the orders, translated into French by IM, setting out measures against the Jewish population in the winter and spring of 1943. Originally published in German and Greek by the Military Commandant Salonica-Aegean or the SD, these are signed by Max Merten and Dieter Wisliceny. Both men were later convicted of war crimes (Wisliceny was executed in Bratislava in 1948). The substance of these orders is reported by IM, and we have chosen not to reproduce the words of war criminals in this book.

The second omission is a short report concerning people who had been subjected to medical experiments while incarcerated at Auschwitz. IM examined these survivors on their return to Salonica in 1944–45, as the doctor in charge of the community's health services. He records brief notes of which the following is typical:

S.V., 28 years old, married
Arrived at Auschwitz on 23.3.43 as part of the first Transport that left Salonica on 15.3.43. Initially worked for five months at Birkenau. It was only in August 1943 that she was sent to Block 10. Five 'injections' at monthly intervals, followed by 10 minutes of X Rays. No longer has periods; suffers from palpitations and hot flushes.

This document makes especially grim reading, with its succinct but repetitive record of medical abuse and its consequences. IM names four doctors he holds criminally responsible for the treatments recorded but makes no other comment. After much reflection, we have decided that it is not necessary to include the report here: its substance is adequately conveyed by the single case of Mrs S. V. noted above.

IM evidently considered the typescript the final version. No manuscript versions were conserved. He made and kept at least one carbon copy. Both the original and the copy were gathered in card folders, where they were held in place by metal clips. Seventy years later, and after considerable handling, both contents and covers are worn. Still, they retain a tangible connection with a man and a time, and so constitute precious items of material evidence.

Alongside these two folders is a small collection of other documents: pages – such as the text translated here as 'The Drawer of the Past' – that did not seem to their author to belong with the main text; photographs from before and after the war, but none, of course, dating from the 1940s; personal letters, including those quoted in the introduction; and some official documents that IM, and later RM, considered precious enough to preserve. Together, they would barely fill an old-fashioned box file: scant traces of a full life of private practice and public service.

THE TRANSLATIONS

Translators are expected to write notes. It is something they do, usually about bits they have found hard to render. But I'd like to make use of the tolerance accorded them to stray from the timeworn path.

But first a few words that are strictly on the subject. The exact relationship of Isaac Matarasso to the language he was writing in is hard to weigh up. It was not his mother tongue, but as a written language French had long superseded Ladino among his educated circle, and he would not have considered writing in anything else. His Greek covered daily and professional needs, but no more. At the same time, since leaving France at the age of 28 he had spoken French mainly in a restricted milieu and with people of the same background. His French-born wife's use of her mother tongue had been similarly narrowed. The inevitable result is stasis, followed by a slow but steady diminution of vocabulary. Meanwhile, in its country of origin, French is busy flexing its muscles, growing and changing, inventing new words, sloughing off old ones. It shrugs its shoulders at the strictures of the Académie Française, adopts *le weekend*, even *le briefing*. In the 1940s IM spoke and wrote in the manner of those he had frequented and read 20 or 30 years earlier. I am sure that this never crossed his mind as a reality, let alone a problem. On the contrary, he writes with confidence, often in short, abrupt sentences that recall the style, if not the tone, of Georges Simenon and Albert Camus, and paragraphs so urgent they seem at times to follow the rhythm of his breathing. Without warning he shifts into the historic present, and his words gain immediacy: it is a reminder that he is describing events that were terribly recent to him and his community, however distant they may seem to readers today. As a translator I have tried to leave him his idiosyncratic voice, without allowing it to interfere with the flow of the story. I have made a point of using only English words current at the time he was writing (not difficult, given that I am outdated myself), and let sense rather than emotion govern the length of paragraphs.

Isaac Matarasso was very conscious of his purpose in writing this account, which he did not think of as 'a book' until well after it was written. He was chronicling events that must not be forgotten. Facts were therefore paramount, and his role was to gather them and get them right. Figures, in the sense of numbers, were important; they represented people, mostly people who had stopped breathing. Statistics at least made them visible.

From time to time the facts become too much for him: when he offers an opinion, one feels it is torn out of him

by a surge of emotion. He asks, 'How *could* you?' He asks
German mothers what they are thinking of when kissing
their children goodnight: why haven't they prevented this
massacre of other innocents? The mothers don't reply: they
are trying not to think about it; they are keeping their heads
down. He asks a friend why he served as a Yes-man on the
council. Word for word, IM writes down his excuses – that
the man held them is a fact, and IM, as a witness, doesn't
judge. Except that he is also a man, a human being with 'a
body that can scream with pain', so he leaps in, in the first
person singular, and the 'I' takes over briefly from the eye.
It helps to be aware of this, to follow him in and out of his
assumed role, to notice when he changes gear.

The more personal the content, the freer his style and
the more readily words come tumbling from him: it is as
though his subconscious memory calls up vocabulary
as needed. It is also true that in venturing where he went
he was asking a lot of language. In the 1940s the words
to describe certain experiences barely existed outside the
professional field; in other cases the events themselves still
lay beyond the bounds of imagination: hence words were in
danger of falling flat, or getting stretched to breaking point
and beyond.

In the Preface, written – as so often – last, he adopts a
manner the opposite of factual, one utterly 'other', which
calls faintly to mind the dream sequences that precede
medieval allegories where the writer, asleep under a tree,
sees his life unfold before him. Here, in reverse, the writer is
visited by those whose lives have been stolen while his own
has been spared. He meets them in a kind of limbo, where
the living are arraigned by the innocent dead, those killed
for existing. The one saving comfort that the writer has to

offer is to step forward himself as their witness and present their case: the pity of it will enlighten and persuade the hard-hearted, while empowering those who love freedom and uphold human rights. It is a moving plea, made by a man described by one contemporary historian as a European humanist, which needs to be heard today and every day. As a writer, self-invented in his forties, he created, in a genre still fluid, a style that opens and closes like a fan according to his changing relation with its subject, and that in itself is remarkable; it also gives his voice its power to move.

II

Early years, late reflections

Isaac Matarasso

This piece of writing is, unlike all the others, a happy bit of serendipity. That we have it at all hinges on a random gesture: a hand once pulling open a long-unvisited drawer. The contents, picked out and examined, set off a slide show of memories now presented for our pleasure, pictures so painterly and detailed that we forget they are made of words. These memories, in clear colours, are from another era; recent horrors do not cloud them, the sky is blue. And yet events of 1943 underlie their reawakening.

The drawer, I am fairly sure, was opened in 1946 or '47. In my mind's eye it belongs to an ordinary table, useful in a hall or study for placing, in passing, one's hat or a book – but it might equally well be a desk. The imagined table has one drawer that opens more or less easily, in which small objects of doubtful use and minor sentimental value can be tidied away and forgotten. The objects in the drawer have lain there undisturbed for many years – maybe since they arrived from Toulouse in a young man's luggage around 1920. He tells us he acquired them at the age of 20 – that is to say, in 1912 – adding helpfully that one of these 'treasures' still smells the way it did 35 years ago, which brings us, give or take a year, to 1947. But the table, how did it survive the war? Abandoned in a house that will have been occupied by German military, then left, like much Jewish property, at the mercy of homeless Greeks in the chaos that followed the Liberation, its chance of recovery by its owners was slim. But the unlikely happens and what is certain is that Isaac Matarasso had available after the war a piece of furniture containing objects bought in France in 1912, postcards too with their messages and dates – not forgetting the 5c. stamps.

67

It was probably after their move to Athens that he opened this drawer for the first time in years. Old furniture in unfamiliar places invites one to renew acquaintance, to find perhaps a different usage for it: what might that drawer be good for? He is delighted to discover this magic carpet which whisks him off instantly to his room in Toulouse and invites his student self to wander round the town evoking in minute detail little snippets of his own and other people's lives. He muses too on the mystery of memory, and so did I, translating words he surely hadn't used or even thought of since those far-off days, words like 'faux-col dur', 'coupe-tifs', 'tignasse' and the splendid 'crayon cosmétique', which allowed a young man to give a bit more substance to his aspiring moustache. Did he meet Andrée at a 'bal musette' – a dance hall? She isn't yet on the scene in these memories suggesting rendezvous on street corners. Words like these allow him and us to measure time and social change: since his years in Toulouse the 'pen-pushers' have turned into the 'economically disadvantaged' – possibly because the pen foresees its own extinction, though he himself still picks one up to correct his typing.

He has called this piece 'Souvenirs', just as others bear the title 'Souvenirs du Ghetto', but there is little else to connect them. The events of the Second World War which are the focus of all his other writing do not exist here. Isaac Matarasso has withdrawn briefly into a more innocent world. The First World War gets a solemn mention, but even today history sees it in a different light from the Second. In 1918 it was to be the last of all the wars humanity had suffered: greater, worse, but similar in nature. The peace, alas, betrayed these hopes, and now we see the Second World War as having its roots in the First. IM's was the generation that, after the useless bloodletting of 1914–18, lost its belief in progress: nothing was safe, nothing secure, and having seen this proved before his eyes, he ends with a prophetic warning. And yet in all that touched on humankind, hope remained stronger in him than fear. There was in this man something irrepressible. However dark the horizon, he invites his readers to keep faith with the divine spark within, and this may well require of us a courage equal to his own.

The Drawer of the Past

A few forgotten objects at the back of a drawer are looking at me. They lie there in the dark and out of mind, like the poor at the back of a graveyard. The world may think them dead, but they aren't dead to me . . . Voiceless, they speak to me.

. . . It was a long time ago. I was 20 years old and it was a hot day. At this hour of the afternoon it is rare to see a passer-by in narrow Baour-Lormian Street in Toulouse.

The tall shutters are closed along the face of its old grey houses. Paving and walls throw back the sun's heat. The silence is as deep as in the depths of night.

I wander aimlessly through empty streets, driven from my room by the heat and the thrilling in my 20-year-old veins. I feel, I hear, the song of the coursing blood, the song of the half-wild animal I am.

A man drifts vaguely towards the street fountain. He presses the spring-loaded knob. Water gushes clear and cold. The old chap appears satisfied.

He releases his clip-on tie from his detachable collar. Takes off the collar in the usual way: first a leftward pursing of the lips for the front stud. Another grimace, with the tip of the tongue protruding, as he feels for the stud at the nape. Ah, that stud! It needs replacing; time and rust have rendered it stubborn; it will have to be changed, but it won't get thrown away – there's a place for old studs in the tin for useless things.

But look! My friend is sluicing his collar in the water!

Now I, like everyone else in that period so sagely stiff and stiffly good, wore a starched detachable collar, the opposite of water-resistant. Wetting one's stiff collar, what a curious idea!

That was the day I learned that celluloid collars had just been launched in France. The novelty that changed the lives of solicitors' clerks, elementary school teachers, the peaceful army of pen-pushers – all those who used to be called the low-paid. The ones we now refer to as the 'economically disadvantaged'.

Oh, sweet unction of the euphemism! You slide into our language with the opportunism of a classy slogan that meets with no resistance – the 'economically disadvantaged'!

And yet there was no celluloid collar in my drawer. Along what labyrinthine mental paths did the tale of the detachable collar make its way into my memory? I can see the chap drying his collar, then putting it back on and clipping his tie into place. I was young and the man was old. He must have been about 40 – that is to say, younger than I am today.

Continuing to rummage, I push aside papers yellowed with age. Postcards signed 'your affectionate friend', 'best wishes from Plan-de-Cuques', 'thinking of you in Blagnac'. Cards in black-and-white, cards in colour, all with stamps at 5 centimes. In the heyday of the postcard one was mindful of one's friends. In the dear old days of 5-centime stamps.

Lying among the papers I come upon a soft crayon in a case. It still smells of roses, 35 years on, and despite being tightly boxed it hasn't lost touch with passing time. But what is it exactly? Ah, I see, it is a 'cosmetic' crayon. Maybe the very object that led my thoughts to the detachable celluloid collar. It must have caught the corner of my eye as I opened the drawer, bringing a train of memories to mind as the day draws in.

Why does man burden his life with the past? A new day should arrive in its maiden freshness, not trailing its winding sheet. Why involve it in the dark labyrinth of vanished years? Why is writing our own story our oldest instinct, so that I see myself in that happy Toulouse past, sporting my little russet moustache?

A young man, freshly shaved, completes his *toilette* by waxing his aspiring moustache. The diligent work of thumb and forefinger ensures that it stays in place, obedient, dutiful, like the hard collars of an era marked by moderation, restraint, scruples.

At this point imagination, which no study has been able to pin down, indulges its vagaries. It unrolls fragments of life – the overspill of a memory that has gorged itself on such food.

Rendezvous on street corners, here a brunette, there a blonde. And here is the blind alley near Berlioz Square known as Les Pénitents Blancs.[25] It is evening now. The white flames of the gaslights project their neutral radiance onto the street, imparting a spectral look to courting couples. An easy-going policeman dawdles past. His eyes are open but his mouth stays shut. For me his little cough has the accent of Toulouse.

A piece of scented wax retains its power to lead the young man that I was back to a dance hall, and to evoke the exquisite lassitude of certain dawns tinged with a roseate hue that has remained unrivalled. The scent too of old-rose, which takes me back to the room in the rue Pharaon, with its antique furniture, faded hangings, Louis-Philippe armchairs upholstered in red velvet, and myself yawning with boredom on a November evening.

It was raining.

I sat waiting.

And no one came to see me.

One last object emerges from the obscurity of my drawer. A stripping-comb.

We are in 1915. *Poilus* in the trenches, relieved at ever longer intervals and unable to shave or get a haircut, employed a kind of comb-and-razor combined, known as a stripping-comb.

This served, by thinning, to reduce the volume of hair on the head. It was enough to run the stripping-comb through the hair to lighten and even it out. Firm pressure would produce an acceptable short-back-and-sides. The great art lay in the neat finish of the sides.

It was easy to end up with unfortunate zigzags, creating a stepped effect.

Then came the bullets and shrapnel and scythed through the ranks of these lads in the beauty of their youth. Stripping-comb in my palm, I salute absent comrades who died facing the enemy.

Life has moved on since those days of wooden crosses. What a host of memories it has trampled underfoot! The left-behind, the dreamers were submerged by the rising wave of a generation that had seen nothing and felt nothing. A generation that had only read the Official Version.

Since then we have been swept into the whirlwind of speed and progress.

We have fallen in love with the new discoveries.

They have turned our heads and left us reeling.

They invite us to keep faith with our humanity, the divine carnivore within.

That's it for today. Time to close the drawer of the past.

III

. . . And yet not all died . . .

Isaac Matarasso

A Conversation with Our Dead

Many of our compatriots are not well informed about your fate or the manner in which you were murdered (and it is chiefly for them that I am writing). Those of our faith all know about it: they have wept over your appalling story and retold it time and again. All have prayed for you. But can one be always weeping, forever praying? Life propels us ruthlessly forward in the struggle for our own livelihood, and above all for that of the very young, the orphans – your children – who cannot defend their own interests.

From time to time on our long and grief-laden journey we pause, let a milestone take our weight and briefly close our eyes. Your eyes are closed for all eternity. In that moment we stand face to face, we and you, the living and the dead. There are too many of you, a vast crowd. And once again we form the words: 'It was an abysmal catastrophe.' The number of victims is so great that some inevitably slip through the net of our pity. And for whom, anyway, should we weep first?

We fall silent, and all around is calm. It is then that figures step forward out of the mass and come to greet us. There they are, in death as they were in life. They start speaking to us:

'My son, why did they suffocate me?'

'Brother, why did the Germans cut short my life? I was young, the future was mine.'

'And you, dear love' – a young woman speaks – 'did you learn what they did to me? I was a walking skeleton when they took me to the gas chamber, I had already suffered so much: exhaustion, hunger, thirst, beatings.'

Then it is the turn of the children from Salonica's orphanages to step towards me, holding out their little hands. Their lips move soundlessly, their eyes speak for them. What can these children have to say?

'Please sir, foreign soldiers took our toys. They tore our pretty frocks and put us in the corner in a pitch-black truck. We were so tired we fell asleep for ever.'

Alas, my God, for whom should I weep first? Their sheer number blunts one's sympathy.

A group of friends step out of the forlorn procession, middle-aged men who had enjoyed the respect of the community. Crowding in on the weary man sitting on the milestone, they plead with him, pressing their complaints.

'Why were we made to journey thousands of kilometres just to be handed over as slaves? Yes, there was an organization in Germany that supplied slaves. If you didn't know that, brother, now you do. It was called the Dienststelle, and had its headquarters in Sosnowiec. Listen carefully. The director's name was Lindner; this 'businessman' sent out orders for slaves to all the occupied countries.[26] In Salonica, for example, Wisliceny, the head of the SD,[27] the man who had us beaten at their headquarters in Velissariou Street, received from Lindner or one of his subordinates an order to this effect: 'Send me all the Jews of Greece'; and it was at Auschwitz that these slaves fetched up.

'Do you want any more details?' I am asked grimly by others. 'Just tell the living how we, the Jews of Greece and elsewhere, supplied Lindner with our gold, our jewellery, our clothes, shoes, spectacles . . . oh, that wouldn't have been much: we gave to the Z.A. (work camps)[28] our labour, our strength. And that wasn't enough. We provided the Dienststelle with our corpses rendered down into super-phosphates, our blood, skin, gold teeth, hair. The speakers fall silent for a moment. Then, before they disappear, one of them asks:

'Are there any antisemites still around, brother?'

It cuts to the quick. I daren't reply. Darkness falls and swallows everything.

Poor dear Jews of Salonica, I have used my weak voice to bring many of the stages of your calvary to public knowledge. As early in fact as 1945 I had given the press notes taken with my son day by day as the events unfolded. Since you have appeared to me again this evening, I am adding your story to the great story of mankind. May your innocence, your martyrdom, serve to calm and enlighten the wicked who foment and perpetuate evil in the world. May it strengthen the generous and free-spirited who respect human dignity, those on whom we base our hope as we endeavour to live on, battling at their side for the happiness of all the human race.

Salonica, January 1946
Dr I. A. Matarasso

Introduction

The Germans occupied Salonica for approximately three and a half years, from 9 April 1941 to 30 October 1944. As was to be expected, the city's Jews suffered greatly under their domination. The German persecutions were rolled out in three phases:

- **A period of partial toleration**, stretching from 9 April 1941 to 11 July 1942, a time of bureaucratic harassment, discrimination, the requisitioning of furniture and the expulsion of certain families from their homes. The Germans imprisoned individuals for reasons often derisory and sometimes for no reason of any kind. There were also some executions by firing squad.
- **A period of oppression**, stretching from 11 July 1942 to 25 February 1943. The planned destruction of the city's Jews began with forced labour. The measures were imposed on 11 July 1942, and a range of odious methods was used to enforce them: insults, humiliations, beatings in public and also in the workplace, starvation rations, complete absence of care for sick or injured workers and, lastly, the profanation and destruction of the famous Jewish cemetery, in use since the fifteenth century.

- **A period of expulsion and destruction**, stretching from February to August 1943. The ghetto was established, Jewish property seized, the community's archives burned. The Jews were herded like cattle into a concentration camp, where the full range of Nazi brutalities was brought to bear, ending with the deportation of about 46,000 Jews out of the city's population of 50,000, crammed into cattle trucks.

Phase One: Partial Toleration

The German forces occupied Salonica on 9 April 1941. It was with apprehension that the Jews watched them take over their city, fearful of the application of the abhorrent race laws. A few days after their arrival the Germans arrested the members of the Jewish central communal council and held them in the cells of the Tmima Metagogon police station, where they were grossly ill treated and subjected to many indignities. Six weeks later they were released. The Chief Rabbi, Zvi Koretz, was away when the troops occupied the town. The Germans arrested him in Athens and dispatched him to a concentration camp near Vienna. He was released and sent back to Salonica in February 1942. In April 1941, by dint of threatening the proprietors, antisemitic elements led by the notorious Papanaoum[29] got notices posted in the windows of cafés, patisseries and restaurants, as well as a few shops and grocery stores, worded as follows: 'Jews are not welcome in this establishment.' This measure was generally unpopular with the Christian population and lapsed of itself in a matter of weeks.

Towards the end of April 1941, all Jews were required to hand in their wireless sets to the Germans. In exchange they were given a receipt with the words: 'Die Ortskommandantur bestätigt hiermit die Übernahme von 1 Rundfunkgerat',*

---

* The district command hereby confirms the receipt of 1 radio set.

followed by two signatures.[30] Periodically there were executions of inhabitants, ten at a time, on grounds of sabotage, arms concealment or communist leanings. In the early days eight of the ten would be Jews, but later eight or nine of each group were Christians. Otherwise, during the first weeks the Germans left the Jews alone. From time to time the local press ran articles in which terms such as 'communists, Jews, free-masons' alternated with 'enemy of the people, accursed race, stateless person' – a selection of equivalents that Nazi dogma had spread around the world by every available means.

From the day of their arrival the Germans installed themselves in comfort. They took over a number of private houses owned by Jews and would later occupy others belonging to Christians. Often they would requisition the apartments complete with furniture, evicting the Jewish family, who were allowed to take with them only their clothes and bedding (mattresses, blankets etc.). Twenty-four hours was all the notice given. Many German officers lodged with Jewish families, well satisfied with the discreet attentions of their hosts.

One morning towards August 1941 some 50 Jews were arrested in their shops and incarcerated in Heptapyrgion prison. They were left there for three months and then released without interrogation. German officers descended periodically on the community offices, spreading confusion through all departments with their shouting and threats. One day the demand was for a list of the wealthy Jews of the community; another day the archives were commandeered; next it was the contents of the famous library.[31] A German lorry would pull up in front of the entrance, and in a matter of hours books, registers, papers and files were loaded up to the accompaniment of shouting, shoving and blows. It often happened that every department was turned upside down in pursuit of a trivial or fabricated piece of information, such as the address of some Jew accused of communist sympathies. On one occasion the council's alleged use of American funds for the purpose of spreading anti-German propaganda was the object of a major investigation.

REQUISITIONS

In May 1941 Salonica's two principal Jewish bookshops, owned respectively by Mair Molho and Chimchi, were shut down, their owners evicted and imprisoned for some months, their businesses forcibly signed over to Christian Greeks – without, of course, any financial compensation. In September 1942 all Jewish stationery shops, wholesale stationery depots, packaging works and printing presses suffered the same fate. Next to be requisitioned were pianos and typewriters. The big ironmongers' shops were literally emptied by the Germans and their owners put in prison. The three Jewish cinemas in the town were put under Greek management after the manner of the bookshops and stationers. The well-known glassware depots of Haïm Benrubi were plundered in an operation stretching over several months.

Since the Germans' arrival, the community had had as its head Mr Saby Saltiel, a choice imposed by the occupying forces. Mr Saltiel had already held the post of secretary during the dictatorship of [General] Metaxas,[32] immediately prior to the Occupation. A compliant tool in the hands of the Germans, and soon snowed under with work and thrown off balance by the relentless stream of orders, he confined himself to obeying the occupiers and satisfying their every wish.

Sometimes, tired and overworked, he sent Jewish petitioners summarily packing. Mr Saltiel was assisted in his 'elevated functions' by Mr Calderon, director of the Hirsch Hospital (and used as an informer by Kirimis, Governor-General of Salonica during the Metaxas dictatorship). Mr Albala, a Jew from Kastoria in eastern Macedonia who had lived for a long time in Vienna, was Mr Saltiel's right-hand man. He too was an obedient servant of the Germans. Both were later imprisoned, then released. It was chiefly during the period of repression (July 1942 onwards), of which we will be speaking shortly, that these two individuals, neither of them of any intrinsic worth, put themselves entirely at the disposal of the Germans, less out of malice than from a mixture of cowardice, stupidity and lack of moral awareness.

During the winter of 1941–42 the working classes as a whole experienced real famine. The poor had to make do with nothing but bread made of maize flour, sesame seeds and carobs: ingredients of cattle cake. During this period the death toll from hunger among the population of Salonica reached tens of thousands, with the Jews among them paying a high price in human lives.[33]

Phase Two: Oppression

FORCED LABOUR

On 11 July 1942 all male Jews aged between 18 and 45 were required to present themselves at 8 a.m. in the town's main public square (Freedom Square). On a day of torrid heat, around 9,000 Jews were drawn up there in close ranks, surrounded by military police from the SS. Latecomers were cruelly beaten. Headgear was forbidden. The Jews were directed in groups towards a nearby office where they were issued with a work card assigning them to road construction. Three hours spent standing in the scorching sun resulted in cases of fainting and sunstroke. Around 11 a.m. the police set about torturing the patient and motionless mass of Jews. SS officers pulled at random a few poor wretches from the ranks and proceeded to beat them savagely while a colleague took photographs. Others were picked out and made to do keep-fit exercises until they dropped from exhaustion. As soon as a man showed signs of flagging, he was brutally beaten with a truncheon on back, legs and head, resulting in loss of consciousness from pain, exhaustion and exposure to the sun. These victims were dragged away; someone threw a bucket of water over their heads and they were left lying in the street. Meanwhile, all round the square and from the surrounding apartment blocks and hotels, German officers and soldiers, young German typists and actors and actresses from Kraft durch Freude* applauded and laughed at the spectacle, while snapping away with their cameras.[34]

Registration of the future slave labourers was exceedingly slow. Those who were waiting were not allowed to quench their thirst, but ordered to stand facing the sun, still bareheaded. Around 1 p.m. they were sent home with orders to return two days later. Several young men already weakened by malnutrition and exhausted from standing for hours in the sun, paid for this cruelty with their lives. Some who did not succumb on the spot died later at home, from meningitis or stroke. On Monday, 13 July 1942, Jews still unregistered from the Saturday lined up again in Freedom Square. This time – on orders, it was said, from higher command – there were no spectators on the balconies and headgear might be worn. But as they emerged from the registration office, every Jew without exception was forced to lie on the ground and roll over and over for some 100 metres, damaging their clothing and sometimes reducing it to tatters. Any who hesitated or were slow to comply were ruthlessly beaten by the SS.

Preliminaries

The dispatching of Jewish men to work sites went on from July to October 1942. Before each detachment was sent, a medical examination took place at the Joseph Nissim Jewish School, where hundreds of candidates were examined by non-Jewish doctors designated by the Medical Association of Salonica. This examination was of the most superficial kind, almost everyone being passed fit for work. Frequently, genuine cases of heart disease, varicose veins

---

* Strength through Joy.

and hernia – even the partially disabled – were pronounced fit. Some doctors did not always square their conscience with their medical knowledge, while the rich often bribed the senior medical officer to exempt them from forced labour. Before leaving, the workers were subjected to a mere pretence at disinfection, consisting of a bath and a short haircut while their clothes were steam-cleaned, after which they went off to the work site. But living conditions were so squalid and overcrowded that within days they were infested with lice and contaminated with scabies.

Enactment

On the roads and mountains of Greece, under a fierce sun, and bent beneath the Nazi whip, Salonica's Jews wore themselves out doing work for which nothing had prepared them. Ill fed, sometimes sleeping on the ground in cattle sheds, without washing facilities or the most basic medical care, a few months sufficed to bring them to their knees. The Jewish community of Salonica (that is to say, Mr Saltiel) issued a summons for Jewish doctors of all ages and dispatched them to the sick. No supplies of bandages were provided and no ambulances. What little quinine there was arrived too late, and several of the doctors themselves contracted malaria. They and their colleagues watched helplessly as diseases worsened and spread. By now there was little more to be wrung from these thousands of Jewish workers, injured, diseased, scabious, ragged and demoralized. Many were sent back to Salonica, leaving a number of their friends dead on construction sites and at roadsides.

At this time the Jewish community of Salonica was once again headed by the Chief Rabbi, Zvi Koretz. He was backed by Mr Saltiel and a Community Council. During September

1942 several meetings were devoted to co-ordinating help for the unfortunates returning from forced labour. Jewish doctors organized the provision of aid at a central dispensary and through home visits. A few vignettes give an impression of the situation.

A convoy of workers, duly announced, is met at the station by the duty doctor and two male nurses. The sick climb down with difficulty, supporting one another in groups of three or four. One man collapses with an attack of acute malaria; another (Pépo Béja) crumples and dies on the platform. We question those in better shape. These young men are grim and recount their ordeal in halting voices: insufficient and unwholesome food, backbreaking work in the burning sun, forced marches to and from the sites and no escape from work, even through illness (any who were unable to get up were left unfed).

One evening the Jewish doctors on call were informed that sick men had been left in a synagogue. They found 50 or so lying on the floor or slumped on benches. One was dressed in his underpants and a coat with no sleeves: he'd sold them to a shepherd to get some bread. Another had nothing but trousers and a vest. Most were barefoot. All were covered in lice. Often they had been camped in derelict buildings in some Macedonian village, or were lodged in byres like animals. Among them were school teachers we had known, accountants, shopkeepers, but the greatest number were survivors of the Italo-Greek war (1940–41), in which almost 4,000 Jews took part, doing their duty as Greeks and as Jews, for Italy was both the enemy of Greece and the ally of Germany, the enemy of their race.

The domestic circumstances of these men were, if anything, more pitiful. My calling took me to the bedside of a workman in the last degree of destitution. He had returned from forced labour to find himself without a job. There was no coal; the soup kitchen served scanty rations; the children were barefoot, ragged and sickly. No family member was in a fit state to fetch the soup, and almost all of them had caught the scabies that their father had brought back from the camp. What a toll of victims among these slave labourers! Death had already thinned their ranks on the job; countless more were to die after their return home.

In September 1942 the Germans decided to lay off the Jewish workers: there was no more to be extracted from these physical wrecks. In any case the winter would put an end to the work. However, with a characteristic twist, they demanded 2½ billion drachmas (100,000 dollars at the exchange rate of October 1942) as the price of this liberation. This sum was duly collected by the community and paid over to the Germans. Property owners, shopkeepers and even the less well off brought their contribution to free the labourers. There followed a period of relative calm.

THE DESTRUCTION OF THE CEMETERY

After putting the living to the test, the Germans set about the dead, ordering in November 1942 the destruction of a part of the Jewish cemetery to allow, supposedly, for a road to cross it. They promised to respect all tombstones dating later than 1912, but in reality, and despite all the pleas of the Community Council, the entire cemetery was desecrated and all the monuments, even the most recent, were destroyed.

Today the extent of the damage can be seen: no tomb has been respected. Vandalism and greed finished the job. Millions of bricks were sold and hundreds of thousands of tombstones randomly dispersed. The city's monumental masons filled their workshops. The tombstones reappeared in sections of pavement and were trodden underfoot by heedless pedestrians. They can still be seen in the courtyard and toilets of a primary school in Filikis Etairias Street. They are even to be found in the precincts of a number of churches, placed there, it is said, out of respect. In fact these churches distribute them to others under repair or being built.

The Jews of Salonica were not at the end of their ordeal. The ghetto would shortly be established; deportation would follow.

Phase Three: Dislocation and Destruction

DEPORTATION

Worst among the Nazi regime's cruelties was the deportation of thousands of human beings far from their homeland. Families were literally pulled apart, children torn from their parents' arms. The horror and pity aroused by seeing these long, slow-moving columns, hemmed in by Schupos,[35] make their way towards the cattle trains ready to deport them . . . what could rival the shame and ignominy of this journey?

In each sealed cattle wagon 70 or 80 people spent eight to ten long days in near-darkness – sometimes more. In the surrounding chaos and stench they had to relieve themselves in tin drums. The hours must have seemed endless. Water was so short that they were tormented by thirst. How can one not see, as in a nightmare, the old man in the back of a truck, dying in his children's arms, the baby struggling in vain to breathe; but no imagination can conceive the unique horror each of these poor people must have suffered.

THE GHETTO

At the beginning of February 1943 it was announced in the papers that all Jews in Salonica were to be domiciled by 25 February in certain specified districts, established as a ghetto. They were strictly forbidden to live anywhere outside this zone. This ghetto already held a large number of Jewish dwellings, as it encompassed all the working-class Jewish neighbourhoods, but a great many Jews remained spread throughout the city in quarters now forbidden to them.

Several thousand people had to move themselves and their chattels into the districts now allowed them. This left hundreds of houses and apartments to be reoccupied by Germans, by refugees from Thrace and by 'friends' of the Germans. I should mention that long before the establishment of the ghetto, large numbers of Greek Orthodox, driven out of Thrace by the invading Bulgarians, had poured into Salonica. The authorities had found it appropriate to lodge the first wave of these unhappy people exclusively in Jewish households, resulting in prolonged overcrowding, although the policy had later to be extended to include non-Jewish Greek households.

Three or four days before the definitive move into the ghetto, German officials visited all the Jewish homes not yet evacuated and seized whatever pieces of furniture took their fancy, thus 'simplifying' the removal process for these families. Meanwhile community representatives pasted up in all the synagogues a plethora of German orders.

Regulations Governing Life in the Ghetto

- A census was taken of all Jews resident in the town, including those whose parents and grandparents had been baptized, and all received a number and an identity card.

- As from 25 February, every Jew over five years old had to wear, as a distinguishing sign sewn to the clothing over the heart, a yellow cloth badge in the form of the six-pointed star known as the Magen David, and bearing the number on the identity card.
- Every Jewish house and flat was to be marked with a Magen David printed in black and nailed to the street door.
- All Jewish shops had to be declared as such, with the inscription 'Jewish Shop' placed conspicuously at the entrance.
- All Jews had to wear the badge even in their own home.
- It was unlawful to sell or dispose of Jewish goods.
- Any citizen buying or having in their possession Jewish goods would be subject to severe punishment.
- Jews were banned from travelling by tram and other forms of public transport.
- All private telephones had to be returned to the telephone company.
- Any Jew found outside the ghetto would be shot on sight.
- No exceptions would be made in the case of Jews married to Aryans, even if baptized. All children of such a marriage would be considered Jews, unless baptized before April 1941 (the date the Germans occupied the city).

The regulation enforcing this last measure was stuck up in the community offices and read as follows:

- With regard to mixed marriages (between Christians and Jews) the Aryan party remains Aryan, while in the case of the Jewish party, all the restrictive measures concerning Jews are applicable.

However, around 15 March 1943 it was learned in the ghetto that three Jews married to German Aryans had been dispensed from wearing the yellow badge and were able to live outside the ghetto. A few days later this favour was extended to other Jews married to Aryan women. There were 16 in all who met these conditions; three of them, however, were arrested on trivial charges and deported to Poland.[36]

The Jews thought that the measures taken by the Germans would stop there. Moreover, in the course of a public meeting held at the Beth Saul Synagogue, Chief Rabbi Koretz announced that he had received an assurance from the Germans that no further measures were envisaged. Saddened and humiliated, the Jews nevertheless knuckled under and carried on with their occupations. They could still go to their work places, even in the zones that were out of bounds; it was just a matter of living in the ghetto.

Ten days later their illusions were cruelly shattered.

Declaration of Assets

On 1 March 1943 the Germans, working through the Council, asked all Jews to declare their assets, both movable and immovable, their deeds and securities, jewellery, carpets, furniture and household effects – in short, everything they owned. Each head of household was responsible for drawing up a declaration of assets in duplicate, under threat of harsh sanctions for omission of items or false valuation. Each had to fill in his own return, to the ridiculous point where the humblest porter was obliged to value his palliasse and his few pots and pans. Thousands of declarations were submitted, which the Germans piled up without a glance. Rumour has it that they were taken one day and deposited in the cellar of Amar's Bank. They are probably still there. The Germans' aim in bombarding the Jews with random regulations was to occupy them to distraction, thus ensuring they were kept on tenterhooks. Taking cognizance of every new regulation, poring over each, discussing, commenting, arguing over such and such an article or unclear detail, and all the while subject to threats of imprisonment or death – such were the preoccupations of Salonica's Jews in March 1943.

The Closing of the Ghetto

On 6 March 1943 the Germans ordered the closing of the ghetto. Seals were placed on all Jewish shops both inside and outside the ghetto. A few days later, their owners were asked to declare the value of their businesses. Once the ghetto was closed, the Jews were restricted to their own quarter, waiting for ever more punitive orders. The great majority worked in other parts of the city. How were they to earn their living? What would happen to their offices, shops, merchandise, factories and workshops? How would they collect what was owed them or settle their debts?

Life in the Ghetto

Sarantaporou Street, the site of the Jewish Community offices, is packed with people, every Jew wearing a yellow badge wide as a hand. They are walking aimlessly up and down, to and fro. No one's mind is on work. How and where is one to work?

The ghetto is now cut off from the market. Some react to the idleness with sullen silence; in others this deadly boredom poisoned by anxiety and confusion results in overexcitement and a spate of words until, dizzy with exhaustion, they stop making sense.

How impotent they are, and how they suffer, all these Jews.

Their eyes turn continually to the windows of the council meeting room in the faint hope of a miracle. Maybe Chief Rabbi Koretz will appear there and give the people tortured with anxiety a few words of hope. Maybe he will say at the last minute that the Germans have agreed to open the ghetto against payment of a swingeing tax. How readily the money would be paid over!

But the windows of the meeting room remain blank.

On 8 March 1943 a certain number of shopkeepers were given permission to open their shops in order to hand over their wares and their keys. They were allowed to retain their papers and the cash in the till. This handover of shops went on for several weeks, though of course only (as we shall see) for as long as the shopkeepers had not been deported.

In the meantime the Community Council presided over by Chief Rabbi Koretz and under the direct control of the Sicherheitsdienst of the SS was organizing life in the different parts of the ghetto.

The Chief Rabbi had to present himself almost daily at the offices of the SD. No witnesses could accompany him. It must be admitted that he had not succeeded in gaining the trust of his flock. Polish by birth, he had been a preacher in a Berlin synagogue when the community engaged him. Yet he had never won the affection of its members, and now, without suspecting him, their hearts misgave them on the firmness of his devotion to their cause.

THE JEWISH POLICE

In the first days of the ghetto a body of Jewish policemen was put together – the *Politofilakes* – distinguished by a yellow armband bearing the word 'Judenordner'. They were charged with enforcing the orders of the SD. These men carried out a variety of duties connected with the community, which gave them access to prohibited zones. They would accompany Jews who had permission to leave the ghetto for a few hours. Each time a Transport of deportees was organized, they assisted the regular police in surrounding the relevant Jewish quarter. They would enter the houses occupied by Jews and get them out into the street, searching for any that might be hiding. The SD supervised this operation. The *Politofilakes* kept order in the Baron Hirsch concentration camp. All were in the service of the Germans. Like their well-known head, Albala, they had little choice but to obey for fear of beatings and imprisonment. Quite a few escaped, thanks to the relative freedom of movement they enjoyed. It was the *Politofilakes* who, down at the railway station on deportation days, the regulatory truncheon in hand, harassed the Jewish flock. Others were themselves hit by the Germans for not being brutal enough with the crowd of unfortunates. Almost all gave a helping hand to the old and disabled, and carried their bundles to the train. At their head, as I mentioned, was Jacques Albala, whose colleague Saby Saltiel had been removed from the Community Council when the ghetto was established. It was Albala's job to translate the orders of the SD and convey them to the 200 *Politofilakes*. He did this with officious zeal and a fatuous authority. As for Chief Rabbi Koretz, his responsibility was to transmit each morning the orders of the SD to the Community Council.

He also ensured that they were carried out, scurrying round and ceaselessly pestering each section, before reporting back daily to the Germans.

Throughout the duration of the tragedy, the community services maintained a febrile level of activity. Chief Rabbi Koretz insisted that employees should work even at night, even on Saturday, and saw to it that the orders of the Germans were enacted with maximum efficiency. Shouting, insisting, threatening, he went from one office to the next. The Chief Rabbi, along with Albala and his *Politofilakes*, carried out his 'duties' with baleful alacrity. The Community Council followed their example. The fear of beatings, prison and death threats stimulated their ardour.

At no moment did the Council attempt in any effective or intelligent way to counter the German regulations. Its members acted as tools of the Chief Rabbi, executing the orders he passed to them with the full force of his authority. He in turn, as the mouthpiece, as we have said, of the SD, lived in dread of the sanctions that would fall as much on him as on his flock.

He may have thought that the anger, the hatred and the ferocity of the Germans would be softened by his obedience and the zeal he employed in preparing and seeing through the deportation. Yet he must have been more aware than the Sephardic Jews that the Germans never show mercy. Had he not been present in person, after being freed from prison in Vienna, at the deportation of the Jewish population of that city? And the setting up of the ghetto in Salonica – did that not indicate to the Chief Rabbi a deportation in the making? Was it beyond him to realize, as did the several hundred intelligent and clear-sighted Jews who later escaped from the ghetto, that even if, as many then believed, deportation did not spell certain death for all, it was a death sentence for a large proportion of the deportees – the old, the infirm, the sick, the children, all those unfitted for the rigours of a Polish winter. Yet this representative of their faith said to his people: 'Don't panic. We will rebuild our community in Kraków. Follow the regulations and orders as posted. No one is to leave the ghetto.'

Here is a document confirming these ill-founded assurances:

Urgent Communication from His Eminence the Chief Rabbi:

We invite our co-religionists to remain calm and collected, to resist any inducement to panic and to put no trust in alarming rumours, given that all such rumours are without foundation.

Salonica, 5 March 1943*
The President of
the Jewish Community of Salonica
The Chief Rabbi of Salonica

This amounted to encouraging the population to fall in line. Could he not have gone about his duties with less haste and zeal? Or found an unobtrusive yet determined way of introducing a little grit into the mechanism of officialdom? Or even got together with some prominent and active citizens to try to partially suspend, or at least slow down, the rate at which these deportations were being rushed along. A slow-down would have been of great benefit.

---

* It should be remembered that the ghetto was closed the following day, 6 March 1943.

Ordinary people always end up coming to their senses, and this community would have got a grip had the rhythm of deportation been slower. Escape routes would have been set up. The initial panic would have given way to a period of calm and reflection. Unfortunately the Chief Rabbi didn't have the stuff of a leader.

THE DEPORTATION BEGINS

Early in March 1943 rumours began to circulate that all Jews were to be deported. It was learned that the railways had received orders to form Transports of goods wagons destined for the town of Brzesko, near Kraków. It was in the Jewish suburb of Baron Hirsch, next to the railway station, that the rumours of deportation were confirmed when the district began to be fenced off with planks and barbed wire. Orders moreover had been placed for a large number of padlocks to secure the doors of the wagons. The suspicions these measures gave rise to were well founded: on 13 March the first Transport of 2,800 people was organized. It was reported to have set off for Kraków on 15 March 1943. This is what took place.

The inhabitants of the Baron Hirsch suburb were 'blocked in' on 13 March: that is, they were forbidden to leave their lodgings. On the morning of the 15th each individual passed through a checkpoint where the identity number on the badge, or star, was recorded along with the wearer's name, and the badge was then stamped to sanction deportation. This was followed by a grotesque farce where each person was required to pass through a designated exchange office and deposit his or her drachmas and other valuables against a cheque made out in złotys, to be cashed by the Jewish community in Kraków on arrival. It was all untrue, as was soon realized, and the story of the zlotys was met with a sad smile at each retelling.

Defensive Reaction

The departure of the first Transport raised the terror among the Jewish population to new levels. The administrative machinery, once set in motion, would grind on until the entire community had been deported. There was no one on the council who dared to contravene the German orders. The Germans published a list of 102 rich Jews who would serve as hostages in the event of disobedience or sabotage. Panic swept through all social classes. There was no visible revolt; no overt act of sabotage was organized. It was private misery and personal losses that were mourned. Each-for-himself was the expression that took root tacitly in people's minds. But to escape was far from simple. Jewish families are large, and the love and affection binding the generations is proverbial. The young might attempt to flee, but how could they abandon aged parents, a sick or disabled relative, alone to an uncertain fate? How plan an escape without enough money, or the help of an honest Christian go-between to get them out of the ghetto and, ultimately, the city. And, once out of danger, how long could they last without any means of support? They also weighed up the risks: the Germans had already caught and shot six fugitives. Despite all these difficulties, risks were taken and sacrifices made. For the Jews of Salonica, Athens, under Italian control and where the racial laws were not enforced, became the Promised Land.[37]

The fugitives, who had to pass through Larissa to reach Athens, enjoyed the protection of the Italian military, who never denounced them to the Germans. The Jews received help and advice from the Italian consul-general, Giuseppe Castruccio, Signor Neri, Captain Merci, another consul, Signor Zamboni, Signorina Capasso, Signor Halit Iero and several other members of the Italian community. It was thanks to the magnanimous activity of all these generous-hearted people and their intervention with the Germans that certain Jews, married to Jewish women who had formerly held Italian nationality, were allowed to leave the Baron Hirsch concentration camp. Thirty families benefited in this way and were directed to Athens under the care and protection of the Italian authorities.

Quite a lot of Jews made it to Athens at the risk of their lives. Others, less fortunate, ended up as the playthings of blackmailers who, after helping them escape from the ghetto, robbed them and left them where they stood. Still others, who had entrusted themselves to so-called protectors, were first despoiled and then handed over to the Germans. Some got to the mountains and joined the Resistance, which in 1943 was still in its infancy in Macedonia. Several hundred brave young men swelled the ranks of these patriotic insurgents after the Occupation of Athens by the Germans. The Jews who made it to Athens were mostly wealthy. No ruse or disguise was left untried in people's endeavours to escape from the stranglehold of the ghetto.

First Transport of Deportees

In the midst of shouting and brutality 2,400 Jews of all ages are herded into closed cattle trucks, jostled and shoved to hurry them along. Why yes, of course, they might miss the train! Sixty or seventy people and their bags are crammed into each truck. The doors are padlocked. The only air comes through small barred windows. Supplies of water run out halfway through the journey. 'How long will the journey last?' 'Where are they taking us?' 'Why?' 'What have we done wrong?'

In the tumult and confusion, mothers search for their children – two, four, sometimes eight in a family. Counting . . . counting in tears . . . The Schupos drive the crowd like cattle. Small children get tossed into trucks. People fall, pick themselves up, collect their belongings, lose their children and cry, ceaselessly they cry. They plead with tears and fume with rage, but to no avail. Everyone must leave, without exception. Ill? Too bad. Can't walk? A stretcher will serve. Even the insane from the Jewish asylum are herded aboard, along with disabled soldiers from the Albanian war – legless, armless, feet lost to frostbite – the blind and the paralytic, pregnant women and 80-year-olds from the old people's home, the children from both orphanages – all are shoved aboard.[38] The methods used are extremely brutal: no mercy is shown. The Transport is finally complete and the doors are padlocked. The train pulls out of Salonica, their home city. Minds hark back to the exodus from Spain four centuries earlier, handled far less barbarically:

In March 1492, Ferdinand the Catholic and Isabella of Castile signed an edict ordering all Jews to leave Spain within three months. They might sell or bequeath their property to others and take with them all their movables, excepting gold and silver. (Leon Dubnov)[39]

A witness report came later that a train of cattle trucks had passed through a station near Belgrade from which came not lowing or bellowing, but the moans of human beings crying: 'WATER! WATER! WE'RE SUFFOCATING! OPEN THE DOORS!

That first Transport set the pattern for all those that followed. Sometimes the boarding was achieved with less brutality. From the second Transport onwards, the community provided food and water for the journey. The International Red Cross was able to supply Baron Hirsch Camp with milk for the children and the sick, together with medicines, but until the last Transport and perhaps the one before, no other help for the deportees was sanctioned. The zeal and goodwill of Mr Burckhardt, a delegate from the Swiss Red Cross, always came up against the same categorical refusal from the Germans.

The Pace of the Deportations

The Jews of Salonica were deported in 19 Transports. The first 16 followed one another at very short intervals (three or four departures a week) and were dispatched in the space of 54 days, between 15 March and 9 May 1943.

There were roughly 2,500 persons per Transport: 42,000 of the 50,000 Jews living in Salonica had been deported by 9 May 1943.

The 17th Transport left Salonica on 1 June 1943. It was said to have been directed not to Poland but to Theresienstadt (Terezín, in Bohemia). This Transport was supposed to be 'favoured'. It was here that the Germans outdid themselves in deceit, lies and treachery. We learned later that this famous 'special' train was directed, like all the rest, to Auschwitz and that the majority of those transported were swallowed by the gas chambers at Birkenau, before being burned in the ovens of the crematoria.

Most of the members of the Community Council (all but three, who would leave on the next Transport, the 18th) had taken their place on this train, accompanied by their wives and children. There were also a number of persons of note in the community, who had worked actively with the Chief Rabbi and under his orders. This Transport comprised only 820 people.

I see them still, those men, intelligent, honest but credulous and faint-hearted, acting with the meek eagerness of the servile accustomed to passive obedience, unquestioning and utterly uncritical, and who strive to anticipate orders so as to carry them out before they are put into words. These men charge into the administrative offices, demanding records, issuing orders, correcting a list of figures here or there, above all berating any employee seen to be a trifle slow: 'God Almighty! Where's your sense of urgency?' For it was a matter of urgency to satisfy the Chief Rabbi, who in turn had to satisfy the Germans, who needed (we found this out later) to supply their gas chambers and crematoria. Oh what a hideous tragi-comedy!

A number of the Community Councillors and notables of the fatal Theresienstadt train had been more or less assured that they would be among the last to be deported, and that even the possibility of leaving a few hundred Jews in Salonica was being considered. I heard the following from a friend, a highly intelligent and actively involved man: 'You ask me, my dear fellow, why I am working with such whole-hearted commitment to the task at hand at this tragic moment in our history. Well, I have a hope which keeps me going: that some part of the community' – he was doubtless referring to the leading figures, as at that time more than 35,000 people had already been deported – 'will remain in Salonica for an unspecified time to administer the community's property.'

He truly believed that. I imagine that other community leaders believed it too. These promises, as false as they were vague, came from the greatest liars, dissemblers and felons the world has ever seen: the small group of SS overseeing the deportation of the Jews of Salonica.

Today my friend is no more than a tiny handful of ashes cast into the wind blowing across Upper Silesia.

THE CONCENTRATION CAMP OF BARON HIRSCH

The Jewish suburb of Baron Hirsch, adjacent to the railway station and converted for the circumstance into a concentration camp, served to corral the deportees brought there from the ghetto for a matter of hours or days. Normally, this suburb was home to some 2,000 people. During the deportation period, when in principle one Transport followed another, between 8,000 and 10,000 were crowded into the camp. There were nights when as many as 30 people piled into rooms just 3 x 3.5 m in size. Many slept in the street, unsheltered from the heavy and freezing March showers. German and Greek guards kept watch round the camp day and night. On the terrace of a house facing the main entrance to the camp machine guns had been set up. Electric floodlights lit up the camp all night. A Jewish *Politofilakis* had been put in charge. This was the notorious Vital Hasson, prompter, abettor and adviser of the Germans in charge of the camp, delegated by the Salonican section of the SS.[40]

The cynical figure of Vital Hasson will remain sadly renowned for his role as oppressor, interrogator and torturer during this wretched period. Himself a Jew, he tortured Jews, holding them in the camp prison in the basement of the mental asylum. He picked out victims at his pleasure and used every possible cruelty to get information. He surrounded himself with a small group of Jewish collaborators, ten at most, and invited the deportees to hand over their gold and jewellery before leaving. Two or three of his cronies did duty as executioners.

Hasson would point out the rich Jews to the Germans, and from early April it became a practice in the camp to segregate any Jews who were considered wealthy. The Germans demanded tens of pounds in gold from them and, with the aid of Hasson, used the most ignoble tortures to extract the whereabouts of their treasure from these wretched men before they left. These practices had become so common that many Jews brought ransoms in gold to hand over to the Germans running the camp to avoid being tortured.

It would take pages to describe the cruelty and sadism resorted to by the Germans in the Baron Hirsch camp, the orgies of all kinds indulged in by the military rabble keeping guard, the outrages suffered by the rabbis, the heavy labour forced on some, the burning of the community archives, the theft of belongings from men sent to mend the roads and all the rest.[41]

A RETURN TO FORCED LABOUR

Before their final dispatch to Poland or some other unknown destination, a further thousand men at least, aged between 17 and 40, were selected, in the first instance from the Jewish suburb no. 151, then from adjacent streets, and finally from the concentration camp itself, where they were separated from their families. These thousand were sent to different parts of Greece, where they spent two to three months doing forced labour. Those who managed to survive returned to Salonica, only to be deported on the last train, which left for Poland on 10 August 1943.

Before going off to forced labour the workers had to pass through the famous 'disinfection', leaving as they went in the precious package put together for the long journey, after which they had their hair cut short and were showered. On boarding the train, they couldn't find their packages, and were told that these were being sent separately: needless to say, the poor fellows never saw them again. Later it became known that they were sold by the Germans and the proceeds shared between them and some collaborators. The workers came back three months later in a state of physical collapse and dressed in rags – sometimes nothing but a filthy shirt. A few brave hearts had managed to escape and reached Athens on foot from distances of up to 200 km. We learned from them of constant beatings and famine rations (mouldy bread and cabbage). The mortality in these labour camps was very high from dysentery, galloping consumption, pleurisy, gangrene and so on.

We ourselves saw these men on their return; they were dazed and exhausted. It was in this state that the Germans loaded them into the last death train.

THE NAZI POWERHOUSE

The nerve centre of the deportation operation was at 42 Velissariou Street, close to the Jewish community offices. Approach was forbidden, and Jewish Police saw to it that the order was obeyed. The organization itself was the Sicherheitsdienst, or SD. It was staffed by men both cynical and cruel, whose names will remain graven in the memories of all who endured their tortures. BRUNNER and WISLICENY were the chiefs of staff. TSITA, or ZITTA, was the executioner. TAKACH and SLOVECK were their acolytes. Their trusted assistant and interpreter was Agop (Jacovo) BOUDOURIAN. A man of no scruples, he served the SD frequently as a spy and invariably as an investigator and inquisitor. A mixture of ferocity and shrewdness, this fanatic interrogated the victims of Velissariou Street with arrogant ill humour but also, above all, with prejudice, translating for his superiors only as and what he chose to, always loading the evidence against his victim.

Well-off traders, bankers, owners of property, collectors of valuables, men such as these were summoned almost daily, and virtually always asked the same question: 'Where do you keep your gold?' And before they had had a chance to reply, the aforesaid Zitta was raining blows on them. Whereupon the victim was shoved into a cell, only to be fetched back some hours later and faced with the same question. If the answer was judged unsatisfactory, the drubbing recommenced. The ruling was always the same: 'You'll come back here, within twenty-four hours, with so much gold – so many carpets – your entire stamp collection.'

It is a fair assumption that the traitor Boudourian got his share of the loot.

The 17th and 18th Transports
The 17th Transport had pulled out of Salonica on 1 June 1943. After that date the only Jews left in the Baron Hirsch camp were those one might call 'privileged' (when compared, that is, with the mass of unfortunates who had gone before), plus what remained of the Community Council, some *Politofilakes*, Hasson and his gang, a few

hundred of the men who were trickling back from forced labour on the roads, the last of the German Schupos who accompanied the Transports, and finally a few poor Jewish fugitives recaptured by agents and brought back to the camp after prolonged torture. Discounting the labourers, there were in all between 120 and 130 people.

On 29 July 1943 the Jews of Spanish nationality, who had been waiting a long time for their repatriation, are summoned to the Beth-Saul synagogue by Wisliceny, officer in command of the SD, 'for an urgent communication'. Most of them turn up. They are told that they will be conveyed to Spain by the means and route available, and that they will be able to take all they possess with them: jewellery and valuables, as well as a maximum of $1,000 in cash per person. But these Spanish Jews have in fact walked into a trap. The synagogue is surrounded by a detachment of German police bolstered by Hasson and other collaborators. The 'guests' are forcibly loaded into lorries and driven to Baron Hirsch camp, where the women and children join them that day or the next.

They were made to hand over all their money and jewellery in individual envelopes, some of which was returned later through the mediation of the Spanish authorities. The Germans then reinvented themselves as rigorous customs officers, going through every package, even pockets, lightening the Spanish Jews of belongings and on occasion suitcases. On 2 August 1943 they were loaded into wagons – relatively clean, but goods trucks nonetheless. One woman, suffering from typhoid fever, asked to be allowed to stay behind until she was better, but this was refused and she too was embarked, along with a Jewish doctor.

It was in this, the 18th and penultimate Transport, that Chief Rabbi Koretz took his place, along with his family and the remaining members of the Community Council. Its destination was a concentration camp in the region of Hanover, Bergen-Belsen. We are now able to piece together the story of this much-discussed Transport of the truly privileged among the Jewish community of Salonica – a story that raises questions from whatever angle one approaches it.

Here it is.

Towards the end of July 1943, the 120 Jews (again discounting the labourers) still lingering in the Baron Hirsch camp were separated into two groups: a rump who would await the remainder left slaving on the roads of Greece, and the favoured, who were to travel with the Spanish contingent by 'special train' to Germany: there was talk of Hanover.

On 30 July 1943 the latest 'guests' – the Spanish Jews just mentioned – were united with their families in the camp. Between 30 July and 2 August a special list was drawn up, the outcome of covert negotiations that had taken place some ten days earlier. The final list was argued out between: 1) the traitor Vital Hasson, head of the camp; 2) Albala, the last president of the Community Council, and his special advisers; and 3) the Germans.* They competed to get their own protégés on the final list: one council employee would figure on the list, another would not. The 74 chosen would

---

* Early in April 1943 Chief Rabbi Koretz had been removed from his position and replaced as head of what remained of the community by Albala. The Germans, having wrung from the Polish rabbi all that his servile zeal, his narrow intelligence devoid of any moral breadth or depth, could give them, had allocated him a small house in the Baron Hirsch camp, where he was living with his family.

join the Spanish Jews on the journey to Bergen-Belsen, leaving Salonica on 2 August 1943. The remaining Jews in the camp, around 150, were to be sent with the labourers to Auschwitz – in other words to the crematoria. The first set would have the further advantage of travelling in groups of 10–17 in a wagon; for the second the rate was 60–70.

The first group benefited also from the unparalleled advantage of going to a camp not organized to kill by gas, machine-gun fire, beating, starvation or medical experimentation. Or at least, not in the section they were sent to. The section appointed to hold our 74 compatriots contained also favoured Jews from other communities, Holland in particular. The Jews from Salonica were housed in compounds, but the advantages they enjoyed were vital when compared with the hellish existence endured by those in Auschwitz and Birkenau. At Bergen-Belsen, in the section housing the 74 in question, the old did not work, and children were not unmaltreated most importantly, they were not separated from their parents. Also exempted from work were mothers with small children.

The fact that in August 1943 the camp of Bergen-Belsen was newly opened enabled some of the Jews from Salonica to get themselves better placed.[42] And whereas in Auschwitz the infamous 'Canada Commando' relieved Jews of their baggage the moment they disembarked, the privileged 74 retained theirs. Of this group 17 members died in the camp or immediately after its liberation. Among these were the Chief Rabbi, Zvi Koretz, and Benico Saltiel, a member of the Community Council.

In September 1945 the survivors from Bergen-Belsen arrived at the frontier town of Siderokastro, not far from Salonica. Feeling ran high among the 1,700 Jews then living in the city. There was widespread talk of lynching, of public retribution, at the very least of a display of condemnation and universal censure.[43]

THE LAST TRANSPORT

A week after the 18th Transport (that of the Spanish Jews and the privileged), on 10 August 1943 the 19th and final Transport took away the Jews who had come back alive from forced labour; they left destitute and in a state of physical distress past all description.

STATISTICS OF JEWS DEPORTED FROM SALONICA

The official list of Transports of deported Jews, as supplied to the Jewish community of Salonica by the state railway company on 29 January 1945, reads as follows:

15 March 1943	1st Transport	2,400 deported
17 March 1943	2nd Transport	2,500 deported
19 March 1943	3rd Transport	2,500 deported
23 March 1943	4th Transport	2,800 deported
27 March 1943	5th Transport	2,800 deported
3 April 1943	6th Transport	2,800 deported
5 April 1943	7th Transport	2,800 deported
7 April 1943	8th Transport	2,800 deported
10 April 1943	9th Transport	2,800 deported
13 April 1943	10th Transport	2,800 deported
16 April 1943	11th Transport	2,800 deported
20 April 1943	12th Transport	2,800 deported
22 April 1943	13th Transport	2,800 deported
28 April 1943	14th Transport	2,600 deported
3 May 1943	15th Transport	2,600 deported
9 May 1943	16th Transport	1,700 deported
		42,300 deported

The three following Transports, of which the above document makes no mention, should be added:

1 June 1943	17th Transport	820 deported
2 August 1943	18th Transport	74 deported
	(The Spanish Jews and the 'privileged'*)	
10 August 1943	19th Transport	2,500 deported
	SUM TOTAL	45,694 deported

---

* The figure of 74 relates to the 'privileged', so the Spanish nationals are not included.

The Last Eight Jews Killed by the Germans in Salonica

It was September 1944, and there were increasing signs pointing to the evacuation of Salonica. The Germans had stopped work on the defences and were already starting to dismantle the existing fortifications – blowing up road bridges and ordnance, dynamiting the main transport intersections, emptying their big stores of clothing and suchlike stuff. The population watched these acts of desperation in thrilled silence, barely able to contain their joy.

The time had come for the Germans to empty the prisons. The first to be freed were the Serbian and Italian prisoners of war; the International Red Cross took charge of them. Among the civilian prisoners were found a few Jews. Jews, still in Salonica? Yes, indeed, a total of seven Greek Jews, a Bulgarian, an American and two families of Spanish nationality were found among them. The last Transports carrying Greek Jews had left in July 1943.[44] Since then, a few Jews in hiding in Salonica and the surrounding region had been picked up by a section of the Greek police known as the 'Death Squad' (Tagmata Asphalias, or Tagmata Thanatou), which was in the pay of the Germans and made every effort to search out these unfortunate people.[45] It was a profitable business for the police, since all the victim's belongings, clothing, shoes, personal items, even gold teeth which were extracted after death, fell to their lot. Objects of more value, on the other hand, were the perks of the Germans of the SD. The thugs in both sections hunted down hidden Jews, drawn by the lure of certain profit. Oh, race laws, what contemptible acts were committed in your name!

Thus it was that in September 1944 there were still Jewish prisoners in the Salonican concentration camp known as Pavlou Mela. As these Jews were few in number, the Nazis couldn't organize a Transport specially for them, so they decided to get rid of them by the most convenient and characteristic method – execution. On 8 September 1944, around 9 o'clock in the morning, the 'Death Squad' of the police, headed by the notorious executioner Dangoulas, arrived at the prison and loaded the following people into the back of a lorry:

1. Lazare Alvo, ill, brought to the prison on 8 September 1944
2. Juda Israel, of Corfu
3. Leon Faraggi, Serbian subject from Monastir (Bitola)
4. Samuel Cohen, of Salonica
5. Riketta J. Israel, of Corfu
6. Rebecca Franco,* of Kastoria[46]

---

* On 1 April 1944, Rebecca Franco, a fine young Jewish woman of 22, was awaiting deportation along with all her co-religionists from Kastoria in the concentration camp of Harman-Kioi, on the outskirts of Salonica. Her Transport was due to leave that very day, when she went into labour. After insistent pleas by a member of the International Red Cross, the Germans in charge of the camp agreed to let this unfortunate woman give birth in a maternity clinic. Her husband was deported. Mrs Franco was delivered of a little girl. The Germans forgot her existence. On 1 September 1944, following a denunciation, the SD imprisoned her. She was executed a week later. The baby was taken in by a Greek family.

7. Simha Moustaka, of Ioannina
8. Julia Gani, of Corfu
9. Fofo Esrati and her child Antonaki, of Salonica[47]
10. Suzanne Saias, of Salonica
11. Haïm Misrahi,* British Palestinian, from Corfu
12. Elie Eskenazi, American subject, from Corfu

All these people were taken to the prison complex known as the 'Clinic Vayanos', where Fofo Esrati and her child, as well as Suzanne Saias, both of whom were cohabiting with Greek Orthodox men, were freed on payment of a ransom handed over to intermediaries in contact with the SD, and said to have amounted to 75 Louis d'or.[48]

In Vayanos prison the men were separated from the women, and all those named above, with the exception of numbers 9, 10, 11 and 12, were treated as follows: they were stripped naked, their clothes were examined, and they were further subjected to the despicable indignity of an internal examination (vagina and anus). They were then told they could put on underclothes or pyjamas and a pair of old slippers. Everything else – clothes and shoes in good condition, watches, rings, brooches, keepsakes of any value – was left in the hands of their persecutors. And in this lamentable state these wretched people were pushed into a van which drove off at once.

It was 11 o'clock at night. A few prisoners were able to follow the proceedings through their barred windows. Misrahi, who was miraculously spared, was an eye-witness and provided the account. The departure of the van was

---

* Haïm Misrahi was spared at the last moment thanks to the intervention of the International Red Cross. As a result he was able to bear witness to these events. He was released from prison on 16 September 1944.

followed minutes later by the rattle of machine-gun fire: at 11.15 eight Jews lay on the ground riddled with bullets.

Twenty-eight other Jews who had escaped deportation but were held in Haidari prison in Athens were freed when the Germans evacuated the city; the SD staff officers had already left. The author of this magnanimous gesture was said to be the last officer in charge, an Austrian. He too left Greece.

The First Account to Reach Salonica

We knew that the Germans had committed a crime, but we were unaware of its extent. The return of some rare survivors and the tale they brought lays on me the obligation of adding what might be termed the epilogue to this tragedy.

In March 1945, after the evacuation of Salonica by the Germans, the 400 Jews of the city who had emerged from their hiding places or come down from the mountains of Macedonia were living from day to day, eking out an existence, in ignorance of what had taken place in the concentration camps of Poland.

We did indeed assume that among the deported, and particularly the children, the old and the sick, a number would have died from cold, hunger and disease, but we had never imagined the appalling fate awaiting the 46,000 deported from Salonica in 1943. And through the long winter evenings, gathered round copper braziers of the kind our forebears used (for we had neither heaters nor furniture), we sat questioning each other and ourselves.

'What do you think has happened to these poor people ... thousands upon thousands of them? Where did the trains take them? What was the point of deporting them? Will we ever see them again?' We all had our stories, focused on particular people – the aged father, a man revered by all who knew him; the husband arrested by the SS in Athens; the wife and children bundled out of a house in Baron

Hirsch camp in the father's absence . . . the two little boys . . . their skipping rope, their marbles. Where are they now? And the inmates of the old people's home who so enjoyed their visitors, and all the children from the orphanage – this man's mother, that woman's orphaned nieces, so old and frail, so young and vulnerable, not one of them spared.

The city of Salonica has been emptied of its Jews: a people honest, earnest, intelligent, if narrow in their views and cautious by nature. An affectionate people, not looking beyond the family circle. A peaceable, law-abiding community that had lost all tendency to belligerence. Four hundred and fifty years of trade, where easy success brought steady returns, had left them sleepy and somewhat sluggish. They had set up more than a score of charitable societies which were operating right up to the time of deportation. How many of these Jews, the 46,000 deported from Salonica and the 30,000 from the rest of Greece, would come back again? These were the questions we were asking ourselves again and again until 15 March 1945, the day when the first witness to escape from Auschwitz concentration camp arrived among us.

His name was Leon Batis, and he was a Jew from Athens. The news spread by word of mouth among the few hundred Jews located in the city. There was no one who was not powerfully moved at the prospect of news of family deported more than two years earlier. It was nearly ten in the evening before I managed to catch up with the man in a café in Megas Alexandros Street.

Leon Batis is a little wary. He looks tired. He wears his hat pulled well down on his head. He observes us with some distrust and a world-weary air. He has come a long, long way. It was December 1944 when he left Auschwitz. Since then he has crossed one country after another, on foot, on horseback and by train. We look at him as one might some strange animal. Questions flow. Journalists swarm. We too beg him to tell us his story. Wearily he answers: 'Again?' It's as though he were saying: 'When, oh when will I be left in peace?' 'Oh, come on, tell us . . .' He says, 'It's a long way yet . . . Athens . . . my family . . . .' Slowly he relaxes; the ouzos help, they loosen tongues. Silence falls as Batis sets his one condition: 'All right, I'll talk, but for the love of God don't ask me questions all at once!

'I've passed through different countries, and more or less everywhere they took me for a madman. That was the first reaction. What I've seen! What I've been through! One day, what you are about to hear will be known and even shown in films and published in pamphlets, and you'll remember Batis, the one you took for a madman. My nerves are shot. However often I tell it, my story still distresses me, when I get to certain parts of my horrific incarceration, but there's nothing I can do. For example, when I repeat in Polish certain words I heard from the Polish partisans who saved me, I feel again the emotion of that moment going through my body like a lightning bolt. Behind me I heard the machine guns and the barking of the SS guard dogs, and in the distance the Polish partisans calling to me. Oh, those voices, I'll never forget them!'

Batis stops for a moment, overcome, but then continues: 'Perhaps I am a bit unhinged. And perhaps too – and this comforts me, if that doesn't sound too cynical – others who come through it, like me, will be unhinged as well!

'I was deported from Athens on 10 April 1944. I was held prisoner by the Germans for eight months. I am happy this evening. It's warm back home; it was cold in Poland.'

There are eight of us, Salonican Jews, gathered in silence round Batis, listening avidly to the tale of the first survivor to get back to Greece.

'There were 2,200 of us deported from Athens on that day. The Germans had crammed us 70 at a time into freight wagons: men, women and children, higgledy-piggledy. The International Red Cross had given us bread, dried raisins and some tinned food. Don't ask me about our journey in those trucks; it fills me with disgust and fury. Like caged beasts half-dead with exhaustion and lack of sleep amid the chaos and the wailing. The journey lasted 11 days, and on 21 April we arrived at the station at Auschwitz – the marshalling yard of humanity. The train stopped, the doors were opened and porters in striped uniforms, under the orders of the SS, burst in. These were prisoners, Jewish convicts.[49] The same fate awaited us. With kicks and riding whips they cleared us off the train. The men in stripes snatched our baggage – it was the last we saw of it. With shouts and blows we were driven, a frightened herd, to be separated into three age groups: (a) those from 14 to around 40; (b) those over 40; (c) the under-14s. Group (a) was to be set to work; groups (b) and (c) were sent by lorry to Birkenau, a camp close by.

'Our Transport, numbering 2,200, provided 527 workers (327 men and 200 women). These 527 were got ready for work: first we were showered, then our hair was cropped, then we were issued with the striped garb seen on others and a pair of clogs, and with that we were slave labour. Not quite, though – a number had to be tattooed on our left forearm.

'We looked at each other: what a pretty picture! Shaved heads like melons. The lovely young Jewish girls – they all had their heads shaved, poor and rich alike. They were in despair. It was the last time they'd bother about their looks. I was told that one little brunette was looking for her handkerchief to wipe away her tears. Her handkerchief? That was in her bag, and the bag was in the hands of the striped devils. A travel bag that had cost her more than she could afford, and filled with woollens bought against the Polish winters. "We are on the way to Poland, to Kraków," they had told us when they rounded us up on the shores of the Mediterranean. Kraków is a fine town, and many Jews live there. Maybe we won't be too unhappy. The Germans were tricking us, as they tricked everyone. And the little brunette kept asking her friends: "Why have we had to come so far? Why have the Germans reduced us to this state? How long will this ordeal last?"

'Three days after our arrival we start work. It's the beginning of our slow death. At dawn we are turfed off our pallets and get up stiff and aching. We're driven with riding whips to where we line up. Any latecomers got beaten by the Germans according to their own unique formula. "Late! you filthy Jew, and why late?" In silence we endured the kicks and blows, and silently replied: 'Why am I late? Why? Because I am a man and it happens sometimes that the species needs a little time in the common toilet you provide for us. Because in former days I lived a comfortable life and was a bit constipated. Why am I late? Because my poor bedfellows (we slept four in a wooden cage) pummelled my back with their feet. Because I had nightmares. Because thinking of the children you stole from me kept me awake. Because I dread the two-hour wait in the cold which it takes to do the roll-call . . . that's hard for those of us who were accountants, watchmakers, teachers, doctors . . .

'A few weeks of work and we could barely stand. The flesh had fallen off us under the diet of soup and beatings, and daily we expected the death blow. There were many different causes of death on offer: semi-starvation led to diarrhoea and swollen legs – legs like telegraph poles supporting a body reduced to skin and bones. Or it might be through pneumonia that one ended on a palliasse in the hospital, a word used to describe the vast rooms filled with three tiers of bunks, real ante-chambers of death; and it wasn't rare to see Kapos killing labourers by kicking them in the chest, the abdomen and, most often, the throat. On our way back from work we often found ourselves carrying comrades killed 'while on service'. We saw section heads shooting so-called fugitives at point-blank range. Yes, we were spoiled for choice where death was concerned, and that's before adding typhus, frostbite and gangrene of the feet, cardiac failure through exhaustion; and the most terrible of all ways of dying, asphyxiation in the gas chambers, through the regular selection processes.'

It was the first time we had heard these terms: gas chamber, selection; we sat stunned. We didn't dare to ask for details. Batis carries on speaking without emotion, taking no notice of ours. He has told the story so often on his journey here. He imagines that everybody knows it. We have to ask him to fill us in on this ghastly subject.

'I told you about Groups B and C, who were classed as non-workers from the moment they arrived. Well, what do you expect the Germans to do with this useless mass? It gets taken at once by lorry to Birkenau, barely 3 km from the station at Auschwitz. Women, children and elderly men are all herded into a vast room, where notices instruct these bewildered and guiltless people in the procedure to be followed:

'"Get undressed. Hang your clothes on the hooks provided. Don't forget the yellow star. Hurry up! Get ready for the showers."

'Whereupon everyone hurries, hangs up their clothes, notes the number on the tag corresponding to the hook on which their clothing (the only belongings left to them) will hang for a few minutes. Then comes the order to proceed into the showers. Each holding a towel, they pass into another huge room where the shower system in place is only for show, as the sole purpose of bringing all the Jews into this gas chamber is to asphyxiate and murder them with hydrogen cyanide.

'What takes place in this chamber of torture and death?

'It is said that death occurs after five to eight minutes of hideous suffering: one cannot get one's breath, it is a slow asphyxiation.

'When this human mass has stopped moving, and when the SS observer judges that the toxic gas has done its work, the doors are opened wide and a special section called the Sonderkommando, always made up of Jewish slave labourers, is forced in by the SS. Its job is to extract any gold teeth and cut off the women's hair. After that the corpses are taken off on trolleys to the lifts which will deliver them to the crematorium.'

It was the first time that we, eight Salonican Jews who had escaped from the German grasp and were now gathered around Batis, had heard such a story. It was indeed unbelievable, and had he not warned us, we would have taken him for some melancholic fantasist.

As it was, I felt that Batis was telling the truth.

My thoughts went to those dear to me, huddled tightly together in a last embrace and kiss. I saw my father. My neighbour saw his mother; another his adorable niece, Esther, and one poor man his two children, Charlico and Stellica. We saw in a flash, in this acrid, suffocating, death-dealing air, the bulging eyes, the constricted throats, the distended veins in the neck. And we heard the short, spasmodic, rasping cries: "Mummy, I'm ch . . . cho . . . king." We saw a whole family clasping one another, limbs entwined, twisted like the growing branches of a vine round its support – their father – then collapsing and dying from the effects of the gas. Then we saw an SS observer, gas mask covering the monster mask beneath, noting on a sheet of paper: "Gas X resulted in death in such and such conditions."

We saw hell on that evening of 15 March 1945.

That scene in the gas chambers played itself over and over, times without number. The powerless victims of the concentration camps knew it well. And it was surely not unknown among a section of the powerful who chose to do nothing and to close their minds. One day they will be arraigned at the bar of history and called on to justify this culpable indifference.

Talk on, Batis, talk on. We looked on hell, and then we saw nothing more, for our eyes were blinded by weeping and Batis became a shadow made out through tears and cigarette smoke, and our pain was measureless, as high as the chimneys of the crematoria at Birkenau. We had no voices left to question Batis. The survivor had fallen silent, apathetic. He has known hell, and has come back; he was an inmate there.

He began to speak again, but only snatches of what he said stayed with us . . . We sat a long time in silence before asking him to tell us how he escaped.

'It was 18 January 1945. We knew that things were going badly for the Germans. During the rare breathing spaces between assignments our Polish comrades, always better informed than we were, whispered words of hope. Suddenly we got the order to leave Birkenau. There were 100 SS running around frantically giving orders, and there we were, 5,000 slave labourers, drawn up and ready to follow them we didn't know where. Picture 5,000 skeletal figures, ill-clothed, many in clogs, others with sores on their feet, in ranks by four, fenced in by 100 SS armed with sub-machine guns. We set out on this gruelling march, 50 km of it. Not everyone was able to follow; some, unsteady on their legs, tripped and fell. From time to time we heard a gunshot behind us and counted one comrade less. An SS doesn't waste time. As soon as one of them spotted a man who fell behind his group, gave signs of weakness, stopping or straying from the ranks, that man got a bullet in his nape. Ah, those gunshots, dry, cold, spelling death, they stiffened our spines and gave us the grit to walk straight.

'Killing the innocent, the weak, the exhausted, killing those who don't want to die, killing men who have been reduced to the condition of starving beasts, those who have no means of defence – that is truly Nazi. Do not forget, repeat it everywhere: there is no people in Europe that deals out death with such passion, such viciousness or such stupidity as the Germans!

'After 50 km we came to a stop. Then we were driven like cattle into open goods trucks, 120 men per truck. Think of the capacity of a goods truck and imagine 120 sick wretches piled in one on top of the other. Many ended up suffocated. We had already lost 500 men during the 50 km march, 500 men murdered. How many died in the trucks? I couldn't say. After a couple of hours the train stopped. We were told to get out and be sharp about it. We were at a station close to a forest. It was snowing. Several of us, without drawing attention to it, had noticed the SS setting up machine guns a few yards from the railway line. Sensing a danger of sudden death, instead of grouping ourselves we scattered and bolted for the forest, followed by a sustained volley of machine-gun fire. I was one of them. Of 4,500 prisoners, I should think 3,000 were gunned down as we left the train. They chased us right into the forest and set dogs on us. I was with a compatriot called Elie Mazza and a Pole. I no longer know how or when night fell. The shooting stopped, silence and darkness enveloped us. We found ourselves in a Polish village, no better than hunted animals. There are days when I ask myself what I, a native of Attica, had done to the Germans, that they should seek my life.'

These 'Supermen' went looking in the hinterlands of Macedonia, that farthest outpost of south-eastern Europe, for young children, ordinary men and women, and the aged, whom they literally booted out of homes for the elderly. They assembled them in Transports and delivered them to the ovens of the crematoria. We know this today, but it needs to be heard over and over again to leave an indelible mark on the history of the world: these monstrous doings, which barbarians would not dream up, this assembly-line death, this death made to order, with its up-to-date accounts, its well-kept books, its balance sheet of human constituents recovered from the crematoria, its assessment of human bodies as the raw material of industry, all the crimes that only this self-styled Master Race has perpetrated in Europe, and which are the hallmark of Nazi ideology. DO NOT

FORGET! These are my thoughts after listening to Batis, the one who got away.

It was midnight when we took our leave of him, and each of us took home his provision of nightmares for weeks to come.

The Second Account

It was less than three weeks after Leon Batis' passage that we heard of a further six arrivals, named as follows:

1. Mr Cohen Menachem from Salonica
2. Mr Allalouf from Salonica
3. Mr Canetti from Didymoteicho
4. Mr Taraboulous from Didymoteicho
5. Mr Soulema from Salonica
6. Mr Calvo from Nea-Orestiada.

These six had been companions throughout their ordeal and made their escape together. They might have been brothers in their mutual affection and support, and hadn't been parted for a single day since their escape in January 1945. All six are strong fellows, tanned, alert, intelligent, on their guard. Their heads are close-cropped. Tattooed on the left forearm of each is the number identifying him as a slave labourer. They find a certain satisfaction in preserving this mark of suffering, which will now and for all time shame the men who made it. The American Joint Distribution Committee (AJDC) took care of them when they passed through Bucharest: they are well clothed. They put up affably with being questioned, and Mr Cohen speaks first.

'It was at dawn on 2 April 1943 that the Transport began to form in Singrou Street, Salonica, and the area around. The neighbourhood had been encircled. The Jewish guards, strengthened by the city police and under the orders of a few SS, were turfing out all the Jews and lining them up with their baggage. Shouts reverberated through the chilly air of the new day. An SS officer yelled: "Anyone left up there? Get them all down, the whole lot. Search everywhere, cellars, backyards, privies." Death threats were the speciality of that despicable traitor Hasson: "Anyone one found outside the ghetto or in hiding will be killed on the spot!"

'A Jewish guard called down from a balcony: "There's a very sick man up here, he's delirious, they say he's got pneumonia. Must we fetch him down?"

'"Yes", came the answer from an SS man, "drag the filthy dog into the street double quick." We watched him come out, propped up by his wife and son, a haggard man of around 40. Dr Varjabedian had visited him the day before, diagnosed pneumonia and told him to take the greatest care as there were already signs of myocarditis. The sick man was trundled off in a wheelbarrow to the Baron Hirsch concentration camp regardless. Having not died there, he was stuffed into the train with the deportees.

'At around 8 o'clock in the morning the Transport set off, crossing Egnatia Street, flanked by Schupos on horseback. It was a huge crowd, defenceless and made up of families of all ages. It was pitiful to see the children with their little legs, unable to keep up, while the Schupos kept on shouting: "Schnell!" Pretty girls from good families, weighed down by their bundles, were dragging their feet like their parents. There were old people shuffling along with the help of sticks, and fellows who fought in Albania, looking flushed and furious. The great throng made its silent way, force of arms in the rear, threats of death to left and right.

'"They're shipping us all to Poland, to Kraków, they say." "What for?" "For the arms factories." "Do they need children and pensioners?" "And the sick and disabled as well?"

'The mothers were the most anxious in that crowd. They never took their eyes off their children, and there was panic if one of a brood went briefly missing. A working-class woman with the good sense of her kind shouted out: "What do you reckon, brother? Supposing they've got us together so they can kill us?" She was met with silence: everyone knows that prophets are off their heads.

'The pavements were crowded with bystanders, Greek Orthodox compatriots, looking on in stunned silence. Not a sign of hostility among them. Quite the reverse: many spot friends in the crowd and wring their hands helplessly. Others shout: "Keep your spirits up! You'll be back!"

'Peoples get along together: antisemitism is not endemic, like skin colour. Antisemites are formed, not bred: Fascists in Italy, in Germany, Nazis.

'The crowd was close now to the Baron Hirsch camp and would be swallowed up within minutes. There we would live amid disorder, dirt and confusion until 4 April. Forty-eight hours of this confinement was enough to make us long to get to Kraków as the Chief Rabbi had promised.'

Soulema interrupted angrily: 'Don't mention that bad shepherd! Since you're talking of Baron Hirsch camp, let me tell you that it's there that I got married. Dozens of marriages took place in that camp. Anything that had approached a promise, inclinations too tentative to be expressed, all took form in this forced intimacy. We were going so far away. Into the unknown. One really needed some protector: a man. And anyway Rabbi Koretz encouraged these marriages. One day at the synagogue of the Monastiriotes (it was in the middle of the deportation period) he addressed the congregation, saying among other things: "The people are giving a true example of courage and composure, and weddings are multiplying. Take heart. We will rebuild our community in Kraków and God will be our help."

'Was the man sincere? Did he himself believe this fairy-tale of Kraków? Maybe his speeches and the orders he issued were dictated by the Germans. That day saw a scuffle when he emerged from the synagogue: a threatening group approached the rabbi's car, and getting him away safely wasn't easy.

'Let me tell you how Rabbi Koretz's promises worked themselves out on that journey,' continued Soulema.

'We left the concentration camp in Salonica on 4 April 1943. I had my fiancée – my wife of a few hours – on my arm. Some honeymoon! Spent in the cattle truck (our nuptial chamber) in full view of 73 busybodies. Lying down to sleep was impossible. We were glad if we could rest and snatch some sleep sitting on our bags with our knees drawn up to our chins. My wife, to whom I had just vowed before the rabbi my lifelong love, was snuggled up close to me. She was crying and asked from time to time: "How much longer till we get there?" Yes, the newly-weds of Baron Hirsch camp did indeed have a very long honeymoon.

'After 48 hours on board, and despite all our precautions, the truck stank. It was three days before we were allowed to empty the buckets and fetch a little water. The Germans kept us covered throughout with their guns. One woman went mad in our wagon. She wanted to protect her husband from imaginary murderers: "Keep clear of my husband," she screamed interminably, "nobody go near him!"

'Around the fifth day several individuals, young women in particular, went on a kind of hunger strike with an unusual motive: they stopped eating in order to avoid having to go to the toilet, if one may use that word of the revolting cans placed at the end of the truck. And as for getting to them . . . But I'll spare you the scenes of despair and the many displays of selfish and shabby behaviour occasioned by the conditions in our moving prison.'

Cohen took over here.

'It was on 12 April 1943 that we arrived at Kraków – sorry, Auschwitz! Oh, what relief! What happiness! We are all standing by our bags, the children round their parents. The newly-weds cling together, pressed even closer by the crush of those around them. Our train has stopped for good. We can't wait to get out, breathe fresh air and stretch our cramped limbs. The welcome from the SS guards is brutal: any delay in picking up one's bags or gathering one's children was met with well-aimed jackboots. – What is it you want of us? Can't you see that the mothers are collecting their children so as not to lose them in the night and the rain? Don't you see that young woman clasping a baby only 25 days old? (She gave birth four days before being deported.) And that poor old man who's just missed his footing getting down from the train? And what about that limping veteran of the Albanian war? No – the SS see nothing but the orders of their master, Himmler. The travellers were exhausted, weak and defenceless – as for the gallant Germans with their guns, what heroes!

'There were 2,700 people in our Transport, of whom 515 men and 300 women were picked for work. We learned later that the other 1,665 were asphyxiated within hours of their arrival.[50] The whole lot were driven off in lorries. This was one of the worst moments of our calvary. We had let ourselves be press-ganged into this wretched journey so as not to be separated from our families, our elderly parents, our small children, in my case my young wife – and now the best part of our own selves is being torn away. Where are they taking them? We look across at the lorries; we hadn't even hugged one final time. Ah, the pain of that moment in the thin, icy rain of that Polish railway station! And the fury! Had we but known!

'We are lined up in fours and marched to Birkenau. A nearby companion in misfortune is caught gazing too intently at the lorries holding his wife and his two kids: he gets a rifle butt in the small of the back. It's quick march and eyes front, and no fretting about the wife with the baby in her arms or the children calling for Daddy. The lorries taking the non-workers, the useless, somewhere in Poland, to a crematorium somewhere . . . don't give them a thought.

'Our company advances through the rain; our guards never take their eyes off us. We keep up the pace and stay in line. We represent a complete cross-section of Sephardic Salonica, dear city now so far away! Quick march, David, the butcher! Quick march, Solomon, the draper! Quick march, Marika, you who were always top of the class at school! And quick march, bank director, and you, well-known philatelist, beaten up in Salonica by the Gestapo to get at your stamp collection! In a little while, bent double under the Nazi whip, believe, if you still have the courage, in a better future, and if the flogging is severe, hope for justice and for vengeance.

'A short march brings us to Birkenau. This is a large concentration camp, known above all for its crematoria, for the number of slave labourers and prisoners to have died there (998 in 1,000), for the size and number of its barracks, the electrified barbed wire of the perimeter fencing and the harshness of its discipline. We were taken on arrival into a vast room and ordered to place on a large table all our possessions irrespective of value: penknife, cigarettes, razor, fountain pen, nail file etc. Then a Polish prisoner tells us, in French first and then in Spanish: "Here you have to forget everything, father, mother, wife, children. Just obey. Now you register." On a large sheet of paper we write name, forename, age, profession, languages spoken, number of gold teeth, crowns, bridges. Finally we have a number tattooed on our left forearm. Jewish prisoners have a small triangle tattooed below the number (there are some Transports where this is not done). It is said that they have never got beyond the number 200,000 but repeat the sequence 1–200,000 as necessary, marking each with a different letter of the alphabet.

'The tattooing completed, we are taken to the cold showers, where we have to rub ourselves all over with an oily anti-parasitic. We also get shaved from head to foot. Of our clothing, all we get to keep are our shoes, which are searched later for hidden valuables. We return to our barracks at the double. This is our new accommodation. My temples are throbbing, and I'm shivering. I'm still wet all over. At the back of the room, where it's dark, I can make out wooden bunks. Oh, if only we could sleep – sleep long and deeply enough to forget, to feel nothing, to believe that all that has happened since leaving Salonica is no more than a hideous nightmare, and never to learn the fate that lies in store for us.

'"Stand to attention!" We form in ranks, and are given black-and-white-striped jacket and trousers, both made of stiff cloth, to which are graciously added vest and underpants.

'"Break ranks! Dismiss!"

'We haven't had time to examine our new uniform before we are called to attention again by the insolent trumpet blare of a Teutonic voice, the sort of voice one adopts when scared on a lonely road at night. The Nazis are for ever yelling to keep up their own morale, perhaps to crank up their courage. The voice is shouting: "Soup!"

'Ah, soup! That wonderful word, learned at a mother's knee, a universal word that knows no barriers of class or place. Hot soup, balm for our stomachs upset by cold, exhaustion and foreboding. We file past the server holding our metal tins and receive, if receive is the word, some faintly warm liquid containing a few vegetable scraps (turnips, swedes, potato peelings). With this we get 250 grams of bread, and 20 grams of margarine. The whole charitable hand-out will merely sharpen our hunger: at this rate, we reckon, we shan't rub our thighs sore on long marches.

'There was no work given to us on the first days. We got to know our new abode and, when night fell, went to bed. Each bunk held two, three, even four workers. We learn to fit in, taking up the least space we can, lying head to foot, and waking stiff in the morning. We dream – when we manage to sleep – of our comfortable beds at home.'

Time passes quickly listening to memories of Auschwitz; a whole hour has gone by and supper calls us to the table. The companions hark back, laughing, to the soup in Upper Silesia, and one of them exclaims: 'No more misery or beatings, brothers. Let the SS take our places, there or elsewhere.' 'Yes to that!' says another quietly, 'but who will give us back the families they murdered?' And indeed, all these survivors are virtually bereft of relatives. They must start life again from scratch. It is true that they are young and courageous and will find their place in the sun, but they will always be haunted by the memory of loved ones lost, and suffer the trauma of their treatment in those concentration camps.

'We start work on the third day after our arrival. We had to be up by 4.30 a.m., and a loud gong ensured we were woken. Late risers were violently ejected from the barracks to shouts of "Schnell! Schnell!" By five o'clock we were all lined up outside and standing to attention, stock-still and stiff with fear, for the slightest relaxation is punished by a beating. The roll is called at five. We often stand motionless in the cold for a whole hour, a stillness more exhausting than movement. Then, to strains of music (ah, work, what fun!), we leave the camp. Passing through the main gate we notice the inscription:

ARBEIT MACHT FREI[51]

'For once the idiots of the SS have injected an element of humour into their cynicism.

'On that first day at work we were on the "Planning Commando", a grand name for navvies charged with levelling the ground in front of the crematorium ovens – and we had no idea they served to carbonize, at an industrial rate, hundreds of thousands of asphyxiated bodies.

'It was unbelievable!'

'We have always been the victims of our own incredulity', replied Mr Cohen. 'In July 1942 in Salonica' (when the Jews were first forced into slave-labour) 'we were asking ourselves if it was possible that the sick were not exempt. "Is it possible," we said, "that labourers can be left wholly uncared for? Is it possible that the Germans don't bother to feed their workmen?" And later, "Is it possible," we asked, "that they are going to deport the entire population, even the sick, the insane, the tubercular, pregnant women, those in labour, the pensioners and war-wounded? And where," we asked, "would be the advantage in deporting a population in time of war? All the roads would get clogged up. It would be inconceivable." But today it is plain to us that what was really unbelievable was our own gullibility. We were normal people and such sophistication in crime never entered our imagination. When the deportations began, a rabbi said to us: "Believe me, my children, the Germans have a religion and a God. Our religion and theirs are not far apart. The Christian Church has worked hard during this war to defend the oppressed and, above all, the Jews. You are well aware of the efforts of His Holiness the Pope to prevent the mass deportation of civilian populations." The good rabbi wished to calm our apprehension. We have seen since that the good intentions and generosity of the Catholic Church were held in check by Nazi cruelty and the stubbornness of the Italian Fascists.

'To go back to what I was saying,' Cohen went on, 'we were taken that first day with the working party of the Planning Commando to the area in front of the crematorium ovens. Right from the start we were subjected to the German whips and boots. You had only to stop work for the briefest moment to get called over by the overseer and beaten black and blue with a stick. The pain had the victim rolling on the ground. This gave the torturer the chance to belabour your back, chest, even head, with his boots. It was tough then to pick up shovel and pick and get back to work limping, bruised and sore! The nearest comrade expressed his sympathy with a quick glance. Oh, those tortures, those beatings! The SS varied them at will. My companion, here beside me will tell you about his memorable day . . .'

'Yes,' chipped in Taraboulous, 'I call it the day of the high-tension cable. One day, hard at work, I got called out of the ranks by the overseer, a hideous, grotesque brute. He asked me out of the blue to hand over the 20-franc gold piece – a Louis d'or. I should explain that one of us – through an infinity of stratagems – had hung on to one of these coins, which would, according to him, be invaluable come the Liberation. Each time we had an inspection in our dormitory, each time we went for disinfection, he swallowed his precious coin, and settled for getting it back 24 hours later. The overseer believed me to be the owner of this coin. For obvious reasons I had no explanation to offer, so I said nothing and acted astonished. It was all I could do. I hadn't got the gold coin and I couldn't betray my comrade. It was then that the Kapo picked up a piece of cable which, being both supple and substantial, became in my torturer's hands a fearsome weapon. I was to receive 20 stripes on the buttocks. I remember counting up to eight, but if I received the rest I didn't feel them as I'd lost consciousness.

'You may not be familiar with the after-effects of such a thrashing. Well, the next day my buttocks were red and blue and hard as wood. It was impossible to sit down. Over the following days I came out in bloated blisters that stained my underpants with blood. I thought I was developing gangrene. It took two weeks for extensive scabs to start forming, and my buttocks . . . entered on their convalescence.'

A doctor ought to write an article on the subject of the tortures used in the concentration camps and the long-term effects of these brutalities. I had been listening for two hours to the accounts of these survivors and trying in vain to imagine how they went to the very limits of human resistance. I imagined with even more difficulty how, thanks to their youth, they survived. I asked them to carry on with their account, while worrying whether there might be some unhealthy curiosity in seeking out the detail of the death of my 46,000 co-religionists. The vague term 'disappeared' no longer exists for me, now that I have heard how they disappeared, and my devotion to their memory grows and becomes more real.

The youngest of the six, Canetti from Didymoteicho in Thrace, picks up the tale. A shy young man, he talks about the sterilization undergone by a number of prisoners in the camps. He himself was the subject of one of these disgraceful medical experiments.

'One evening four SS officers blew into our barracks and picked out young men aged between 15 and 30. We were taken to a special building where, after a superficial examination, a doctor subjected us to a number of X-rays. I found out later that some of the group had been operated on and had had either one or both testicles removed. For a week we were relatively well looked after, after which we were taken to a laboratory where we were told to masturbate to have our sperm examined. In view of our reluctance to comply, we were given a forcible massage of the prostate with an instrument made of ebonite. After these services rendered to German science we were taken back to our quarters and went on with our dog's life like the rest of the prisoners.'

Canetti suffered greatly. Today he is a young man of 23 and in good health. He remembers having weighed 30 kg. One day in despair, unable to endure further the tortures of the SS, he wanted to volunteer for the gas chamber. It was thanks to a certain Dr Paul, a Czechoslovak Jew, that he was crossed off the condemned list. Dr Paul was shot during a forced march on the route to Breslau [Wrocław], unable to drag himself any farther. Canetti said it was common to see prisoners at the end of their tether waiting impatiently for the arrival of Dr Henkelei, in charge of sorting out the prisoners destined for the gas chamber.

'How can you not long for death', asked Canetti, 'when you are weak, exhausted, reduced to half your proper weight, and on top of that subjected to unimaginable tortures, like the "door torture"? I was put through that. One day, after some minor infringement, a Kapo made me put three fingers of my right hand between the edge of the door and the frame from which it swung. He then slowly closed the door increasing the pressure on my fingers till I was screaming with pain.'

Taraboulous took over.

'On 25 November 1943, at Jaworzno, 26 prisoners were condemned to be hanged: 20 Jews and six Christians, all Polish. One of the condemned men had the time to direct a few words to all the labourers who had been forced to attend the execution: "Friends, we tried to organize an escape route to save you from further torture. The tunnel that we had dug with such effort was the symbol of our liberation and the beginning of our vengeance." He was shot at close range, and his companions were made to hang one another while their judges looked on with hatred in their eyes.'

Allalouf then told us how after two months at Birkenau he was moved with other Salonicans to the coal mines at Jaworzno.[52]

'In July 1943 there were 1,250 men from Salonica at Jaworzno; by January 1944 there were only 58 of them left. The rest had died of illness or exhaustion, or had been selected at one of the fortnightly inspections for the gas chamber. Among my companions in misfortune at Jaworzno, I recognized Leon Frances, the chemist Ammir, Davico Bengorado, Ascher Botton [all dead]. Likewise I remember having come across at Birkenau Albert Segoura, who died of typhoid, Chimon Alval, Leon Amaradgi, Sintov Allalouf, members of the Community Council [all dead].'

Canetti and Soulema describe the heroism of a young woman from Salonica. Soulema happened to be on duty one day at the station at Birkenau.

'The Transports from Salonica were arriving one after the other. A girl, whose name I don't know,' said Soulema, 'was so horrified by the brutality shown by one SS towards the deportees as they were disembarking, that she stabbed the officer. She was shot on the spot.'

Canetti added that 1,600 women from Salonica were killed that day. 'They were transported to the gas chamber packed half-naked into lorries and we heard them sobbing and screaming. The words that stayed with us were, "Save us! They're going to burn us!"'

We could have listened longer, several hours indeed, to the tales of these men, but what we had already learned would never be forgotten. And as for the six witnesses sitting there in front of me, they will be recounting their time spent in Poland for as long as they live, and the story will be passed down to their children's children. May those who have a heart and a God cry out with loud voices should further atrocities ever be inflicted upon Jews: 'Stop this massacre! Don't forget that we are Christians!'

After the Atrocity

Pour qui a vu les ruines du Ghetto
Les faits humains ne sont pas à refaire
Tout doit changer sinon la mort s'installe
Mort est à vaincre ou bien c'est le désert
Paul Éluard*

The Baron Hirsch concentration camp, known for its sorry role as the site of an appalling sum of physical tortures and moral suffering, now lay silent and abandoned. Not long after, the small houses were pulled down and the demolition materials bought for next to nothing by the traitor Nikolaidis, who resold them immediately at a huge profit.[53] Today nothing in the suburb remains intact except the synagogue and what was once the mental asylum, and those two only because they were being used by the German transport company Schenker.

Once the Jews were gone, the Jewish suburbs they had left stood empty and abandoned: notably suburb no. 151 and those of Kalamaria, Regis-Vardar and Aghia Paraskevi. The first two were put out to tender by the Germans and sold to entrepreneurs for demolition. Today there are only ruins. Yet they could have been used

---

* 'They know who have seen the ruins of the ghetto / These human doings must never be re-done / Change must be total or death will take over / Crush death or see the wilderness move in'. From 'Dans Varsovie, La Ville Fantastique', *Poèmes Politiques* (Paris: Gallimard, 1948).

to accommodate the refugees from Thrace, providing homes for at least 15,000 people. There would be a good case for taking proceedings against the speculators who instigated the sale of these suburbs and enriched themselves through their demolition. The synagogue of suburb no. 151 and the beautiful Beth-Saul Synagogue were also pulled down.

There were left in total some 15 Jews married to Aryan women: Greek, German, French and Italian. They had been granted the favour of not being deported, and the official certificate confirming this read as follows:

> The Jew X married to the Aryan woman Y is exempted from restrictions laid on Jews of Salonica who are Greek subjects, such as the wearing of the yellow star and living in the ghetto, and this for as long as the marriage lasts.

However, no shop already confiscated from these Jews was returned to them, nor were they allowed to pursue any legal commercial activity.

Early in 1944, one of these 15 Jews, whose wife was of Italian origin, had the great misfortune to lose her after she gave birth. The Germans deported the husband, leaving their eight-day-old infant, a little girl, 'free' in Salonica. Naturally, all the worldly goods of this unfortunate Jew were confiscated and his house was ransacked.

These few Jewish men – a tiny island – stood powerlessly by, witnesses to the destruction of all Jewish property, the product of the honest work of generations. The wealth, shops, offices, workshops and factories owned by Jews were put by the Germans in the hands of managers: it was a free-for-all. These managers in their turn bought major commercial firms and businesses for derisory sums.

A number of collaborators and informers in the pay of the Germans made a fortune from this windfall. Thus Papanaoum got himself awarded all the tanneries and leather depots.[54] A man devoid of scruples and on the German payroll for ten years or more, Papanaoum knew the Jewish business world of Salonica like the back of his hand. He had a lot of influence with the SD and played a principal part in the measures taken against the Jews of the city. He is even thought to have pressed the Germans to exterminate the entire community without mercy, indicating the Jews with the largest fortunes and giving advice as to the best warehouses to raid. He was the first and worst of Salonica's traitors. He has since taken refuge in Berlin, but before he left, he used his malign influence to get the 15 Jews still in Salonica deprived of the life the Germans had, in a moment of amnesia, accorded them.

THE ASSETS OF DEPORTED JEWS: WHAT FOLLOWED

Following a law promulgated by the Greek government in the spring of 1943, the Germans set up an Administration Service of Jewish Properties (YDIP).[55] For each Jewish business the YDIP drew up an inventory before the administrator took over. The content of the inventory was invariably drawn up in bad faith and to the disadvantage of the deported Jew. Only a minute proportion of the merchandise and fittings were listed, and these were valued ridiculously low. In general, the businesses thus handed over were subsequently run down by dishonest or incompetent administrators. As for blocks of flats belonging either to individuals or to the community, these were managed directly by the YDIP, which pocketed the rents.

When the deportations finally ceased – they had been extended to cover the whole country in October 1943 – there remained in Greece some 7,000 Jews who had escaped them. At the Liberation, in October 1944, around 500 Jews were living in Salonica. Of its Jewish population of 50,000 it is estimated that 46,000 were deported.

The few hundred Jews who had returned to Salonica by January 1947 met with huge difficulty in recovering their property. The YDIP raised every imaginable objection to satisfying the claims of the 50 or so shopkeepers who presented themselves. And what did they find on gaining access to their place of business? As a rule, an empty shop where not only the stock but the shelves on which it had been displayed had disappeared. In a few cases, the owners were able to recover some meagre remnants of their wealth.*

CENSUS OF THE JEWISH POPULATION OF SALONICA[56]
Record of dispossessed families and unmarried persons: 1,125.

Sexes

Men	1,025
Women	559
TOTAL:	1,584

---

* Early in February 1945 the YDIP gave permission for the Community Council to manage its own assets. Today it can collect the rents from the few shops and offices not occupied by the public administration. These revenues go to support communal services, to provide a little help to those in difficulties, the indigent and the sick, and to organize religious practice.

Ages

From 0 to 8 years	42
From 8 to 14 years	49
From 14 to 20 years	161
From 20 to 50 years	1,212
From 50 to 70 years	104
70 years and above	16
TOTAL:	1,584

Occupations

Merchants and shopkeepers	238
Employees	195
Labourers	125
Artisans	244
Doctors, lawyers	21
Miscellaneous	74
Technicians	59
Housewives	155
Schoolchildren	91
Students	18
TOTAL:	1,220

Of the above, 670 are unemployed.

Status

Families	670
Bachelors	620
Spinsters	309
Widowers	215
Widows	90
Orphaned of father	1
Orphaned of mother	1
Orphaned of mother and father	2
Illiterate	135
Property owners	217
Disabled or tubercular	21
Pre-tubercular	21

How They Escaped

With the help of the Resistance forces	353
Hidden in Athens	328
Hidden in the villages of the interior	51
Hidden in Salonica	61
Escaped to Palestine or the Middle East	98
Returned from various concentration camps	733
TOTAL:	1,624

In November 1947 the Jewish population of Salonica numbered 2,200.[57]

SUMMARY OUTLINE OF THE GENERAL SITUATION OF THE JEWISH COMMUNITIES OF GREECE IN JUNE 1947

The Jewish population of Greece, which before the war numbered more than 75,000 people, today, after the German persecutions, does not exceed 10,000, representing a loss of 87 per cent of its members. The communities of northern Greece have been the hardest hit. That of Salonica, which comprised before the war a population of 56,000, today consists of only 1,800 people.

Of the present total of 10,000 Jews, 2,000 returned from the concentration camps of Germany and Poland; the other 8,000 escaped the persecutions by staying in Greece, and only a few dozen left the country for the Middle East during this same period. Today the Jewish population is spread throughout the 19 communities recognized by the Greek government. Before the persecutions, northern Greece had another five communities which have disappeared as a result of the general decimation. The largest Jewish communities of Greece are now the following:

1) ATHENS	4,000 members
2) SALONICA	1,800 members
3) LARISSA	620 members
4) VOLO	560 members
5) TRIKKALA	360 members

It is to be noted that the Jewish population is today concentrated in the large towns, principally in Athens. Most of the survivors find themselves today in a very difficult position, both financially, and as regards professional rehabilitation and accommodation. Of the survivors, 60 per cent have been unable to take up their former occupations. This majority has turned to occupations different from those in which they worked before the war, either because they have not been able to recover their businesses and machinery, or due to a lack of the financial means that would enable them to take up their former livelihood. At the same time, 10 per cent of the population remains unemployed. The persecuted have not been indemnified for the loss of movable property; as for the immovable property, this has been returned only *de jure*. There follow certain family statistics relating to the Jewish population of Greece.

Marital status

Single	3,770
Married	3,430
Widowed	1,100
Divorced	30

In the 'single' category above, those who are not of an age to marry are omitted.

Age

1–5 years	Male	305	Female	300
6–15 years	Male	460	Female	420
16–20 years	Male	370	Female	340
21–60 years	Male	3,905	Female	1,770
60 years and above	Male	340	Female	240

Orphans

1) Orphans aged 1–5 years

Orphaned of father	23
Orphaned of mother	2
Orphaned of father and mother	2

2) Orphans aged 6–15 years

Orphaned of father	50
Orphaned of mother	7
Orphaned of father and mother	150

Status and/or Occupation

Housewives	2,910
Schoolchildren	1,070
Students	105
Merchants	500
Shopkeepers	260
Miscellaneous	1,830
Pedlars	240
Labourers	320
Private sector employees	576
Government employees	54
Farmers	10
Others	120
At the orphanage	38
At the old people's home	22

Professionals

Doctors, Dentists, Veterinarians	40
Lawyers	12

Engineers	24
Agricultural engineers	10

Women without protection
There are about 500 women and girls with no means of support.

Health
Five per cent of the Jewish population suffers from tuberculosis or is predisposed to this illness. Two to three per cent suffer from chronic or contagious illnesses.

Financial Situation
Forty per cent of the Jewish population are without means. Fifty-four per cent manage with much difficulty to cover their living costs. Thirteen per cent live decently, and two per cent fall outside these categories.[58]

General State of the Communities
The antisemitic measures of the Germans also affected synagogues and graveyards. The synagogues have not only been pillaged; the majority have been totally demolished. Ten synagogues have been wholly destroyed, and ten others have been demolished in part.

As for the graveyards, six have been totally destroyed, five partially destroyed and seven are in good order. Today only six or seven synagogues are in a fit state to function.

Before the war, the buildings belonging to the above communities (their communal property) will have been worth around $400,000. Today, at least $50,000 would need to be set aside to cover minor repairs to these buildings.

There existed in Salonica before the war 2,500 private businesses that were seized during the Occupation from their rightful owners. Of the 300 for which a claim has been filed, to date 150 have been returned to the title-holders.

Education
There are nine Jewish schools in existence, but only four function, owing to a lack of staff and equipment.

Jewish Press
The following newspapers appear in Greek fortnightly:

1) *The Jewish Home*, published in Athens;
2) *The Jewish Tribune*, published in Salonica.[59]

However, a shortage of financial underpinning makes their future publication problematic.

Laws Concerning the Jews of Greece*

1) Law 367/45 regarding the reorganization of the Jewish communities and the institution of the General Council of the Jewish Communities of Greece.
2) Law 2/44 and 337/45 regarding the abolition of the anti-Jewish laws decreed during the German Occupation and the restitution of Jewish fortunes.
3) Law 808/45 complementing the above laws.

---

* Information from the Central Council of Jewish Communities in Greece.

4) Law 846/45 regarding the abolition of the right of the State to all possessions of Jews without heirs, and the ceding of this right to an organisation set up to assist the general and economic rehabilitation of Jewish survivors of Nazi persecution living in Greece.

5) Law 1029/46 regarding matrimonial questions between Jews etc.

All Did Not Die

The Jews remaining in Greece today escaped deportation, risking death at every moment. During the period of extermination they took refuge, in the strictest secrecy, in all manner of hiding places – remote mountain villages, concealed rooms, hospitals, old people's homes and mental asylums, and in the few areas held for a time by the EAM-led Resistance.[60] In all these cases the support of the Orthodox population played a vital role. (Countless vicissitudes, dangers and sacrifices were undergone in order to lie low in some hiding places. Some were the victims of informers who threatened to denounce them to the Germans: the blackmailer had to be bought off and a new place of safety found, also at a premium.)

The general health of the survivors reflected the hardships suffered since their escape. Families had been torn apart by the process. A father might find himself with two children, his wife having been deported with the third. Elsewhere only a single member of a family survived . . .

The Community Council reconstituted in Salonica after the Liberation is now overwhelmed by the problems it is facing. Returning Jews want their former homes back, but given the large influx of Orthodox refugees into these areas, the Greek authorities maintain that it is hard to accede to their demands.[61] Whenever possible, Jews are allocated one room per family in houses not their own and in districts unfamiliar to them. Housing difficulties are set to increase with the gradual return home of Jews who found refuge in Athens and those making their way back from Poland, nearly 1,000 in all up to the beginning of November 1945.

The Salonican Jews who escaped from the ghetto and were missed by the round-up operations are free but wretched. They are also among the war's true victims, lacking in everything: clothing, bedding, furniture, pots and pans, money for their immediate needs. The help they are given is insufficient, often insignificant and always ineffective. They need a massive advance of funds to enable them to return to productive work. Ensuring economic viability will also bring a corresponding lift to morale.

The various organizations dedicated to helping war victims have not yet considered the problems of Salonica's Jewish community. There are so many issues to resolve. How will livable conditions be established for the deportees returning in small groups? What is to happen to community assets or to the property of those who do not return? If whole families have perished, who is to inherit their assets? Who will help the surviving Jews to recover?

These are today's agonizing problems.

Since the preceding passages were written (in January 1945) the Joint has brought effective support to the Jewish population of Greece.[62] It has established an orphanage, a centre for those with latent tuberculosis and a home for young girls, and found places for a few older people in a home. It has set up a medical relief centre and a loan fund, is placing people with TB in sanatoriums and has organized children's holiday camps. The Joint has continued the great, beautiful Jewish tradition: 'Pick up and help those who fall. Give of your heart and your strength.'

Epilogue

The events we have set out in these notes speak with a tragic eloquence.

They cry out in pain, they howl with rage.

Each fact and observation is a dagger thrust in the conscience of all humanity, of whatever race.

They should alert, awaken and disturb those who today pronounce themselves happy.

Let us not forget that during the First World War the Germans, with the agreement of their allies, promoted the killing of a million Armenians in Asia Minor.

No one is unaware that during the war that has just ended, the SS caused the death of 6 million Jews.

As for the hundreds of thousands of Christian civilians murdered by the Gestapo in different parts of Europe, it is impossible to put a precise figure on them.

One day new 'supermen' may single out other races as 'inferior' and decree their eradication.

We must beware.

Lightning strikes at random.

Disasters give no warning.

Be on your guard.

We all have a part to play in preventing further cataclysms from engulfing mankind. Each one of us has a body that can scream with pain, whatever race or country we belong to.

IV

From the Salonica Ghetto

Isaac Matarasso

The six short pieces of this section – mainly brief evocations of the weeks spent in the ghetto – were the first written by Isaac Matarasso about the events of the Occupation. Five are dated 1943, and, as he was very precise in the matter of dating, I take it that these were written in the vanished weeks between late March and the unknown date when he and Robert were arrested and thrown into prison. In that uncertain reprieve, when grief for his aged father was sharpened by an understandable but misplaced feeling of guilt at having left behind him in great peril his closest friends and the community to which he belonged, he pauses to pay tribute to the few and the many whom he feared – too rightly – he would never see again. Two years later the full horror stood revealed and, having recovered the cache of papers left with his wife during his 18 months with the Resistance, he turned tributes into elegies by adding a brief farewell to those commemorated there.

These chapters are his most personal pieces (apart from his evocation of student days in Toulouse). Only here does he allow himself an active presence, watching, listening, talking, once even making a joke – though one has to read it twice to notice it. He is introducing us to friends, to companions in misery, in one instance to his torturers. Only in this last is his focus on himself. In all the others he is simply the facilitator, the one who gives to others their voice: in quiet conversation with close friends, in the noisy, frightened free-for-all of a crowded household, in the reverently observed portrait of the rabbi with whom he'd had probably little more than a professional acquaintance.

The description of his interrogation by the SD was written in that brief space before events lose their immediacy and narrative takes over. It reflects the first sifting of experience in the light of reason, an experience we can only be grateful not to have undergone.

It is to these texts that one turns most eagerly when looking for the man. He speaks here with the voice we hear in his last letters. He brings to vivid life the scenes, the occasions and the people he describes. It would be hard to read these chapters without emotion, and yet he had never written anything before except articles for medical journals sharing his professional observations and experience. And so protective was he of what he considered personal to himself and others, and so little did he prize his writing skills, that he held these pages back from publication, showing them only to a few close friends. (Some chapters were passed, after his death, to Jewish publications, where they were accompanied by affectionate tributes to their author.[63])

The first five pieces come complete with their context. They present a situation before embarking on the story. If there is an interlocutor, Isaac Matarasso introduces him (it is in each case a man). The account of his own sufferings at the hands of the SD is impressionistic in style, and remarkably effective, for one come newly to this kind of writing (though even the postcards sent to friends in his twenties clearly sought to entertain, and as surely succeeded). The last of the six, 'The Liberation', written no doubt in 1945, is different in starting baldly with a story told in the first person by an unnamed narrator, raising inevitably the question: is this a venture into fiction? The *possibility is reinforced by an uncanny similarity to IM's own experiences, as though he had drawn on these in writing it. The reality, much simpler, has recently come to light thanks to the research of Dimitrios Varvaritis, who found a version published posthumously in Le Judaïsme Séphardi. This text has small departures from the typescript, including, at the end, the words: 'Ainsi me parla un mien ami, employé de commerce, un rescapé.** This, then, is another piece of reportage. We might have guessed that IM, that modest man with his passion for truth, would not have embarked either on fiction or on covert autobiography. Instead we meet him once more in his chosen role of witness, the intermediary for individuals whose voice would otherwise be silenced, the storyteller for a community. The account given him by the friend rediscovered in tragic circumstances in 1945 becomes a moving illustration to the dry pages of statistics, to the reports drawn up and the work done by Isaac himself in the year that followed the restoration of Greek rule in the city: this, it says, is what awaited the survivors on their return from Poland, from the mountains, from hiding in cramped quarters, from fear and danger and death: it was, astonishingly, not so very different from what had preceded it.*

By the time I knew Isaac Matarasso at all well, 15 years had passed since the events recorded here. In one way or another they had been processed. I can only say, as witness to the witness, that I never saw in him any sign of anger. When Robert once overstepped the mark in a letter, it was

---

* 'This I heard from a friend of mine, a commercial employee, a survivor.'

his mother – who very rarely wrote – who sent him a stinging reply. Miraculously, his father's love for that 'divine carnivore' humanity came through the fire purified. Had he found an SS man lying bleeding, it is my belief he would have bandaged his wounds.

Mordoh Pitchon, Teacher

Several thousand Salonican Jews were taken by the Germans to carry out repairs to the roads in the mountainous hinterland of Greece.

This is July 1942.

In these dry and dust-ridden parts of Macedonia the great scourge is the sun.

These makeshift labourers dig the ground, carry stone, pushing and pulling heavy loads.

The work is back-breaking.

Thirst is intense, water rare.

These men are labourers, artisans, shopkeepers, pen-pushers, accountants, teachers, lawyers and so forth.

Two months of forced labour, suffering, want and deprivation have been enough to leave most of these slaves on their knees.

How much longer is this to last?

Mordoh Pitchon, teacher at the École de l'Alliance Israélite, has come back, burning with malarial fever.

He stands in front of me, covered in cuts and sores.

His head has been shaved. His eyes are sunk in their dark sockets. He is pale, no doubt anaemic.

His voice broken, he tells me that he can't go on. He has been 'laid off' for a few days.

He rises with difficulty, takes a few steps, bent, shrunken. A looking-glass reflects his sharpened features. He stares in horror, finding it hard to recognize his own wasted face. He addresses his reflection:

'What a sight I am! How repellent! Is that you, Mordoh Pitchon? You, the teacher of literature, the devotee of the French classics?'

His weeping rises from the depths to which the Nazis have reduced him. He comes back to me and collapses on my shoulder, sobbing . . . I hold this son of Israel fast, as if he were my own son seeking refuge on my breast. I hearten him and promise to look after him.

'I'll dress your wounds. You can stay here. It isn't you who are despicable, my dear Mordoh. It is those savages, those Antichrists, those expert murderers. Some of them say that we killed Jesus, but it's they who torture him daily and will end up killing him for all eternity.'

I saw Pitchon frequently. He imagined, dear fellow, that my medical skills extended to other realms of human knowledge. He even believed, when the deportations started, that my advice would give him protection against the Nazis, that I would be untouchable.

Mordoh Pitchon was a former ward of the Allatini Orphanage. Certain alumni of the Alliance Israélite Universelle had had him admitted to the orphanage when he was still quite young, and he had received a good education in Paris at the École Normale Israélite Orientale.[64]

He was one of those intelligent Jewish children of Salonica, disinherited by fate but rescued by a good fairy, sheltered, cared for and schooled before being launched in the world to spread education, truth and moral values among the Jewish masses of the Near East.

Mordoh sits opposite me at my table after a family meal. He is freshly shaven, his hair still very short. He remains

170

thin and extremely pale. This pallor, the deep-set, dark-ringed eyes and the gentle, melancholy smile are what now come to my mind when I see Mordoh Pitchon. He looks his 30 years; with his head inclined to one side, he softly recites some lines of Verlaine for my 15-year-old son:

> Dans le vieux parc solitaire et glacé
> Deux formes ont tout à l'heure passé . . .*

and

> Votre âme est un paysage choisi
> Que vont charmant masques et bergamasques . . .†

In the course of the evening we went to sit on the hill known as Sheik-Boujou, which dominates the city, and contemplated in silence our beautiful town, so familiar and so greatly loved.

'My God,' said Mordoh, after a long pause, 'what will become of us? We are among the last Jews in Europe not yet entirely wiped out by the Germans.'

He feared what was to come.

There was already talk of a ghetto.

By February 1943 we were all penned in there.

Mordoh recovered his calm. He was looking out across the plain towards the Vardar and the horizon, where the marshes flamed like molten gold.

---

* In the deserted park, wintry and chill, / two figures came and walked and are now gone.
† Your soul is a landscape, delightful of itself, / to which masked dancers add a further charm.

Mordoh had that melancholy smile particular to fine-looking young Jewish men, a forgiving smile. It's the resigned smile of the wise man surrounded by a hostile and threatening crowd, who takes God to witness and looks with seeming pity on these sinners.

The light was fading.

Down below us, barely 500 metres distant, we contemplated in silence our vast and famous cemetery, its destruction under way for the past few weeks.

This too was the work of the occupying power.

We sat in silence for a good while, unaware that our thoughts were running on the same track.

Mordoh, to my surprise and as though continuing a conversation broken off, suddenly said:

'Yes. That's where they lay, just days ago, our luminaries of the sixteenth century who travelled here from Spain. And see, over there is the old cemetery where we stopped burying a hundred years ago.'

I picked up the thread and carried on:

'And look at those thousands of marble containers, Mordoh, lying pell-mell in the wreckage.'

'It looks like a general departure, a grand exodus, doesn't it?'

'As though absent travellers had left their luggage behind.'

Was this the signal of an everlasting wandering?

Was it the warning sign of our utter destruction?

So it was that we continued talking until nightfall about our dead who enjoy eternal peace, and about the living victims soon to be gathered together in the ghetto.

Our two souls were as one.

We had only to fall silent in the darkness to meet on common ground.

We were following the road trodden by millions of sons of Israel, singing the same song of grief and hope that lifted us out of ignominy into the sublime spheres of Jewish spirituality.

I shall never forget that evening, my dear Mordoh Pitchon, vanished now in the smoke from an Auschwitz chimneystack.

Life in the Ghetto

Within half an hour, this street in the ghetto, where chance has reserved a room for me, will lie spellbound in apprehensive silence. For now, a few pedestrians, almost all men, are walking steadily up the dilapidated road.

It's odd to see the swaying motion of these anxious Jews: body leaning slightly forward, a see-sawing from the hips with each step . . . right, left . . . right . . . left, like grandfather clocks, pendulums weighted with the sadness of passing time. Pendulums out of true, heavy with the past, panicked by the present.

It's still cold in Salonica in March. Evening draws in swiftly, and most of the windows are closed. The curfew will follow soon, when no Jew may move in the streets. One is glad then to go home, to be with one's family, in the comfort of feeling that our miseries are shared. The children, under their mother's wing, are waiting for the head of the family, who will bring, as every evening, snippets of bad news and a few sweets for the little ones. This is the best moment in the day of the ghetto: the time when we stew gently in our misery, stirring the pot of memories, worrying in unison, comforting one another.

All the Jews of Salonica are going to be deported to Poland. No hope remains. Three transports have already left, with Baron Hirsch concentration camp providing 2,500 Jews for each.

All week the talk has been of unlit wagons with padlocked doors, of the lack of privacy within and the great length of the journey. We will all have to spend innumerable hours in these prisons on wheels and each of us calls up his own nightmare.

Dread is in the atmosphere around us. Even the smallest ones, like sparrows, sense the thunder in the air and huddle against their mothers.

Every father has a haggard look. What pitiable heads of household! There has been no reaction yet, but what can they do? Where should they escape to? And how, with the kids in tow? And those bright blue eyes and brighter black ones, those pretty heads leaning on a shoulder or falling sleepily against a chest, set the parental tears quietly flowing.

Someone coming in from the street brings his burden of worries home. But is this really home? No one is at home in this large hall with five rooms opening onto it. They shelter six families, comprising twenty-eight people in all, plus two Aryan girls, maids from Bulgaria, with no clear grasp of the calamity that has overtaken their employers.

This is home to no one, and yet all fraternize.

All will suffer the same fate: from old Mercada, maundering on at the end of the corridor as she warms her hands at a brazier, to the baby young Sarah is suckling by the stove. Both mother and child are fair-haired and blue-eyed. That doesn't make them Aryan, though. They will be deported.

Everyone is back now. It is seven o'clock, and no one may leave the house until morning. All have a Star of David sewn on the left-hand side, over the heart, in accordance with the injunction issued by the SD from their headquarters at 42

Velissariou Street. The youngest children are exempt. Little Aronico is throwing a tantrum. He's jealous of his brother, Albertico, who is eight years old and wears the star, the historic badge.

The usual crowd has gathered in the hall. No one can hear himself speak as everyone talks at once. The clatter of cooking pots and the hubbub of children playing, running, falling over, combine with the racket of voices to heighten the state of tension and anguish.

The heads of family are the most to be pitied: they don't know what to do to save their children, wives and aged parents. They can only talk – talk without end, argue, split hairs, try to guess the outcome of their ordeal. Grandstanding, they talk on and lose track of what they're saying.

Some are prey to an indescribable anxiety which reveals itself in gloomy silence; others, driven by manic excitement, jabber away until thoughts grow incoherent and heads spin.

'What will we do in Poland?' 'Is it very cold there?' 'Jews there speak a different language from us.' 'How will we get on together?' 'Why are the Germans taking us to Poland?' 'Why are they moving us so far?' 'It's to make use of our labour.' 'Yes, but the old people and the children, they serve no purpose, so why deport them?' Someone throws in: 'It's to wipe us out.' 'Why go so far, then? Would the Germans have had a problem with killing us here?' 'The crime would be too gross,' someone else replies.

The women start to cry, the children copy them, so the pessimists and spreaders of bad news come in for criticism.

We're tired.

We've had our fill of talking.

And of listening.

The 28 tenants are all present. It is nine o'clock. A heavy silence falls: they might be waiting for the Last Judgment. The silence drags on, interrupted by a long, lugubrious moan filling the void above the weary heads. It emanates from old Mercada.

The voice of the old woman is heard, as it might be in a dream.

'God wants to put us to the test.'

'God wants to punish us.'

'We have not obeyed his commandments.'

'We shall all perish and the Messiah will come.'

Somebody shushes old Mercada.

The night hours tick by. No one makes a move towards bed. Here and there children have fallen asleep, on a chair, on a sofa or on the floor. Their mothers shepherd them carefully off, carrying the youngest in their arms and singing snatches of old Spanish lullabies. Finally they get tucked up and kissed.

German mothers too are familiar with that sublime gift: the goodnight kiss, calling down a blessing on those little heads. What are they doing back there? Why haven't they prevented this massacre of the innocents? The children of the world are part of one great human family, knowing no frontiers and no prejudice.

A great calm reigns now in the hall. Just three men and their wives are left. All are silent. One can hear the ticking of a clock and, from time to time, a snore from Samuel, the neighbour at the back, a tall, thin man who never says a word. He hasn't spoken since the first news of the deportation; before that he was a great talker, the life and soul of the neighbourhood.

'Can't he be quiet when he's asleep too?' comments one of the group.

Samuel's eloquence when snoring is indeed remarkable.

There – Samuel has just stopped.

'Good! A little moderation, Samuel.'

With Samuel a trace of comedy lightens the night's oppressive atmosphere.

Now silence engulfs the watchers once again. Outside, in the street, the tramp of nailed boots on the roadway; in the house, a child's whimper. The couples separate to watch the next instalment of their fears played out in nightmares.

At the SD Headquarters, 42 Velissariou Street

They made me stand, nose to the wall.

Endless hours pass.

I am forced to hold this rock-like pose, for fear of getting my forehead banged against the wall by Tsita, the group's sadistic torturer.

Half-dead with tedium and fatigue, I pass the time by watching the blurred shadow of my nose slowly lengthening.

Doors open with protesting squeaks, or slam shut, jarring my spine, sole support of my exhausted body.

When a door squeals I picture some fawning collaborator bringing the boss a tip-off.

When it slams I know that a man on duty has just left.

I've been standing like a fence post for longer than I can now work out. I have to force my memory to situate myself in time.

Let's see: this morning at eight a well-built SS officer dragged me here by my coat collar. I waited my turn in the little inner courtyard of the Gestapo.

There was a brusque call from the traitor Hasson. I'd hesitated. Shortly after that the colossus appeared. Hasson had pointed me out.

It was at that moment that I was grabbed and dragged like an empty barrow behind this bruiser puffing at his cigarette, and . . . wham, he threw me like a parcel at the feet of his superior, clicked his heels like an automaton and disappeared.

What did they want with me? What was I accused of?

I was given no time to speak in my defence before I was being whipped, punched and kicked.

My screams drowned out their voices. When I drew breath between brayings, I heard orders, cutting, angry, noises like *Chlah* . . . and *Nach*.

I was interrogated. Someone translated.

The interpreter, a bilious-looking Armenian with a little black moustache, whose greenish features I made out through my swollen eyes, shouted: 'Answer! Come on, answer!'

I muttered a profanity, an insult through clenched teeth, then more loudly: 'Finish me off, if you want, *but I've nothing to say.*'

The beating began again, harder and faster. I was knocked out; it felt as though my head was splitting, and I crumpled.

Time's sands were passing through a vast hourglass.

I raised myself on one knee.

Everything was going round and round. There was something oddly comic about the sight of circling furniture. I seemed to be sucked into this spinning movement. Grasping at air, I fell forward again face down.

My interrogators too were swinging round me in a continuous ellipse, with their insignia on their chests, their piggy snouts, shaven heads, thick necks and navvies' hands. They were doing a jig that swung them from floor to ceiling, ceiling to floor.

The whole thing was idiotic. A tune filled my aching head. An accordion was playing. I thought I saw Edith Piaf;

I smiled at her . . . pathetic . . . ridiculous. Perhaps I was already mad.

Oh, the pain, the pain! The world is still revolving, and the monsters as well . . .

They can't beat me any more, they're turning too fast. I can see them passing.

'There goes the oaf with the whip,' I force out indistinctly: 'You can't lash me any more!'

I move out of the orbit and slip away.

'That makes you furious, doesn't it? You can't reach me now!

'You are going to turn for all eternity, you're already in hell. I shall be redeemed through your sins.'

My knees were bleeding, my eyelids swollen, my sight was blurred, the shadow of my nose had darkened, my mind was a jumble . . . My mouth was filled with blood, the taste acrid and salty. And always the awful giddiness.

Tears, blood and bile. I felt sick, feverish.

The ordeal was unending.

I wanted to kill! kill! kill!

I found myself standing again . . . I'd been standing for ever, since time began.

All is quiet. A sunbeam chilled on the ghetto roofs strokes my ear and neck. A buzzing fills my head.

The horizon (the wall) leaves me numb. I close my eyes . . . to see and hear better. My head is like a sawmill where belts and blades spin faster and faster. The horizon meanwhile has turned into a vast, pinkish desert.

The sudden scrape of a chair on the floorboards breaks the silence. Someone behind me has got up and is approaching.

My tense neck, every nerve alert, feels the breath of Brunner (the boss).

This is it: he is going to have more fun, amuse himself knocking my forehead against the wall . . .

Bang . . . bang . . . bang . . . head buzzing . . . red desert . . . vertigo . . . the wretch bursts into laughter. I am a wounded animal, good for the chop.

'I may die soon, who knows. I'll never shop my friends . . . they're good men . . . I'll see you spinning in hell for all eternity, and you won't be able to lay a finger on me . . . ever, because I'll be at the feet of a judge who will crush the lot of you, swastikas and all!'

Harbi Haïm Habib

Tonight, as every night since they penned us in the ghetto, Harbi Haïm Habib has been keeping prayerful vigil.

He has organized Selichot services.

He comes every morning to the community offices.

There is always a crowd outside, waiting impatiently for news. It mills and eddies round the community's building in Sarantaporou Street.

When Harbi Haïm Habib appears, it parts before him.

The old man's tread is steady. His height and pale complexion mark him out.

A few friends question the rabbi about his flock. He scarcely replies. He himself knows nothing. Chief Rabbi Koretz and the SD are better informed He can only pray. He simply repeats:

'Patience, my children. God will not abandon us.'

His role in the community at this time was minimal. The Beth Din, of which he was an influential member, had been disbanded by the Germans. In any case, its business was no longer relevant. Who has the heart now to sue a neighbour, or seek a divorce? It was marriages, on the contrary, that were being celebrated quickly, anywhere and by the dozen.

Harbi Haïm Habib presented a strange yet noble figure.

He was at once the most orthodox and the most lenient of the rabbis in Salonica. For a long time he served as deputy to the Chief Rabbi, a role he filled with great dignity although it was not to his liking.

He was a modest, unassuming man, yet a great expert in the Torah.

His library was famed, and his judgments carried weight.

He disliked the title of Chief Rabbi, particularly when it fell to him to represent the community in any interaction with the authorities.

It also involved being present at celebrations and receptions, and he disliked protocol. He neither could nor would bring himself to conform.

How could he be expected to offer his hand to a lady?

He refrained.

This attitude is said to have made a very bad impression on one occasion, where the wife of a Consul had courteously extended her hand to Harbi Haïm Habib, who felt constrained to ignore the gesture.

It did not conform to the Torah.

In the same way he neither ate nor drank at receptions organized by strangers, for what took place at parties did not always conform to the Torah.

He was scrupulously righteous, and would sometimes torture himself with the thought that he might have done something wrong, that contravened the Torah and the will of God.

Some of his actions had about them a touching naivety.

The shop of a modest cobbler burned down one night. Next morning Harbi Haïm Habib presented himself with words of comfort and encouragement as the cobbler had no fire insurance, and then proceeded to ask whether his own shoes had been mended before the disaster.

'Yes,' replied the cobbler, 'but they were burned to a cinder.'

'Well then, I must pay you for the leather and other materials, since you had to buy them for me.'

He would even attempt to pay the conductor twice over for his ticket on the tram, on the grounds that he'd got off recently without paying.

When he received a woman in his office, he would leave the door wide open and ask her to speak quietly.

Oaths were taken before him.

I can still see him standing by his table, his tall frame erect, his expression grave.

On the table lies the Bible and in front stands the man about to swear on the Torah that he has or has not done such and such.

At this point Harbi Haïm Habib closes his eyes with thumb and forefinger of his right hand and declares in his firm and unmodulated voice: 'My son, before you lies the Torah; the Torah of the Lord and of our fathers. Take heed and let your heart speak.'

Whereupon with raised voice he proclaimed: 'Speak the truth!'

At that, all lies and evil thoughts beat a retreat, vanished before the holy man who hallowed the air they breathed and placed the oath-taker firmly in the presence of God.

Nobody lied in front of Harbi Haïm Habib.

He always refused to assume the Presidency of the Beth Din.

He was never more than a member of that assembly.

He feared to be mistaken, to commit an injustice, for only God is just and he alone is Judge.

He rarely attended the principal synagogue, Beth Saul. He might be met with any evening at the small and modest Carasso Midrash, founded by Esther Carasso, grandmother of Maître Emmanuel Salem and my own great-grandmother. This Midrash, at the bottom of a little garden, was a quiet place for meditation and well suited to the modesty of Harbi Haïm Habib. The good rabbi prayed there. Truly he spoke with God. He gave the impression of being out of the world and in close communion with heaven.

Such was the gentle, just and learned spiritual leader who was to find himself, like every other Jew, confined one day in the Baron Hirsch concentration camp.

He entered without fear.

He took with him his entire fortune: the best volumes of his treasured library.

He lived in crowded rooms, without privacy, like everyone else.

When he walked in the camp's narrow streets, people lowered their voices and spoke softly. Silent and gentle himself, he inspired respect and during those days gave courage by his presence.

Someone once commented that there was in him the inner quality that is gifted to those destined to take their place beside the throne of the Eternal.

He advanced slowly and slightly bent, turning his mild and compassionate gaze on the people who drew back to let him pass. One woman said: 'Look at him! He's like a scroll on the move.'

In the camp he kept silence, praying by the hour.

Sometimes, to entertain the troops, Guerbick, the SS commander in the camp, would order the traitor Vidal

Hasson to get everyone out in the streets and make them dance. Any who didn't dance were beaten.

It was said that Hasson himself balked at subjecting the rabbi to this humiliation.

On another occasion Guerbick ordered the streets to be swept. The women were to do the sweeping and the head of the SS himself gave the order that Harbi Haïm Habib was to help them.

The poor man was preparing to obey. It might be a divine trial he deserved – for who is without sin? Broom in hand, he stood waiting. A group of women hurried over to extract their rabbi from this degrading situation. Harbi Haïm Habib tried in vain to prevent them.

The day of deportation arrived, at last.

Harbi Haïm Habib was eager to leave the camp where he had suffered so much from watching others suffer.

Several volunteers carried his bags to the death train.

A trunk with his books was put in a dark corner at the rear of the wagon.

The rabbi and his family entered the prison on wheels.

He was murmuring the Shema.

No doubt he recited it at his last gasp in the gas chamber at Auschwitz.

Blessed be the memory of Harbi Haïm Habib.

In Memory of Dr Joseph Amariglio

The Vardar blew all night long. It rattled shutters, set stovepipes squeaking in their rusty wire collars and wailed as it caught on the sharp edges of corrugated iron roofs. It was a cold night, and for Dr Joseph Amariglio it had been a sleepless one. In the nightlight's glimmer he looked at his four children and his wife, crowded into a single room by the promiscuity of the ghetto. He was sombre, his mental landscape invaded by horror. Soon, perhaps as soon as tomorrow, all the Jewish residents of Sarantaporou Street – the street he lived in – would be deported, along with those of the streets round about. He saw himself, with his wife and children, forming part of the grim convoy. They would be held briefly in the Baron Hirsch concentration camp, and then they would be deported, like the rest of the Jews of Salonica.

He looked again at his wife, Emma, her expressive eyes shuttered by their heavy lids, her face drawn and pale. At the back of the room in the shadow stood two beds, with two children in each. He could hear the childish breathing, regular and quiet. His gaze drifted over to the beloved heads for whom he, the father, was responsible. He would be the one to endorse the move to Poland, or else to organize their escape across country, to some village in the mountains. He knew that any Jew found outside the ghetto was shot on the spot. Hadn't he just lost his friend Cohen and two other Jews who were trying to escape? Confusion set in: he could come to no decision. Risk-taking was beyond him. He loved his wife and his children with a great and equal love. If only he could risk his life and not theirs!

Through the misted windowpanes came the hint of daybreak. In silence and with infinite care Joseph extricated himself from the bed, put on his slippers, covered his balding head with a skull-cap and cast a last glance at the sleepers, his whole estate. Leaning towards them, as though in an unconscious sign of willing and loving submission, he seemed to say: 'Sleep peacefully, my darlings, you'll have your breakfast soon, I'm going to get it for you right away. Sleep on; back in a minute.'

He closed the door and went to the kitchen. As he prepared to light the stove with charcoal I too got up. I had found the night long and was glad as I lay in bed to hear someone moving around; one poor wretch is glad of the company of another. My old friend Joseph was bent over, puffing his cheeks and blowing the coal and resinous wood into flames. He didn't hear me. He put his heart and soul each morning into getting breakfast for his family. It was as though by this solicitude he lessened their fear and worry. Up the tin pipe over the fire shot a crackling spray of sparks. Joseph straightened up, satisfied. I gave a little cough to announce my presence. He turned and embraced me as he had each morning since we had become ghetto brothers. I smiled at him, taking in his fine head – the brilliant complexion, blue eyes and fair, curly hair framing the high forehead. Everything that morning conspired to give my friend an air of kindness, gentleness, resignation and serenity. For the first time I understood that ritual sacrifice performed each morning.

We talked about the night just past, the rough wind, the street noises, the neighbour's shutter which had been banging before daybreak. All these trivial details brought us close. Each of us in his room had been lying awake thinking of children and relations. Like my friend Joseph, I too spent the night seeing the long columns setting out for Poland through the frozen mud, harassed by guards who had exchanged the cross for the whip or the truncheon.

While he waited for his children to wake, my friend Joseph sat down in a corner. A movement of the head from left to right spread slowly downward until his whole body was swaying like the pendulum of some old, long-suffering clock. Joseph was praying.

Oh, that interminable swaying of Jews in despair, of the Hassidim at prayer; the swaying that both comforts and exacerbates. Its monotony wears the look of resignation. It narrates the incidents, the pogroms, the antisemitic movements instigated and sustained down the centuries by Christians, sometimes unwitting – customary, recurrent, commonplace. Yes, like an old pendulum stubbornly and hopelessly persisting in its monotonous oscillation, my friend Joseph swayed to and fro without finding peace. No Christian, however good, will ever understand the depths of pain and rebellion expressed in this despairing rhythmic motion during prayer. No, he cannot understand: the movements will strike him as ridiculous or grotesque. Yet there are, rising in the minds and hearts of these Jews at prayer, confined in ghettos or penned behind barbed wire, waves of revolt that go rippling outwards to earth's farthest bounds. Who sows the wind reaps the whirlwind.

At length Joseph got up and left the kitchen carrying breakfast on a big tray. I went with him. He seemed to take pride in accepting the lowly role of maid, even deriving from it a private joy. I opened the door to let my friend pass. His wife was still asleep, her head fallen on her breast. The children were awake, talking in whispers. I closed the door behind the ministering father, and went to wash and dress, and then to resolve the pressing problem: organizing the escape . . .

The occupants of the house (five rooms for five families) were beginning their day. When I knocked again at my friend's door everyone was up and the beds, still warm, were airing. In the far corner, facing east, his head and shoulders covered by the tallit, the tefillin wound round hand and forearm, Joseph was reciting his morning prayer. Now bending from the waist, now straightening up, now leaning towards the book, now drawing back, he was murmuring prayers of which I caught fragments: 'To you I will give the land of Canaan as an inheritance', and then, 'Touch not my anointed ones, said the Lord, and do my prophets no harm [Psalms 105: 11,15]'.

I refrained from making my presence felt: it would have been disrespectful to God before whom Joseph was standing. As I listened, I heard him beating out the rest of the prayer in a voice shrill with pain:

'God of vengeance! Eternal One, God of vengeance shine forth [Psalms 94:1–2]. Rise up, judge of the earth, give to the proud his deserts. Deliverance belongs to the Lord; your blessing is upon your people [Psalms 3:8]. Selah. The Lord of hosts is with us; the God of Jacob is our stronghold [Psalms 46:11]'.

Joseph was not normally given to public observance, but he was a fervent believer, reading and commenting on the Bible in Hebrew. During our childhood years at the school of the Alliance Israélite Universelle he was the favourite pupil of rabbi Tazartes. Once he had taken off his tallit and tefillin, I asked him why he was marking this particular day with a religious ceremonial. 'I don't know, Isaac,' he said, 'I don't know any more. I wanted to talk with our God, to pray, to recite the Shema, to implore him to save his people, and to ask forgiveness for all our sins. He will hear us; my heart is less heavy this morning.'

Joseph starts putting his stamp on some sheets of paper as he does each morning – his prescriptions. Today he is stamping more than usual. 'You're expecting to "sell" a lot of prescriptions today, Joseph. Business is looking up in the neighbourhood!' In fact since we've been in the ghetto, we've been treating almost everyone free, and it was Joseph who spent the most time with the poor. He knew how to talk to them. He'd had a lot of practice.

•

My friend Dr Joseph Amariglio was transported to Poland with his wife and four children. They let themselves be carried away in the horror and confusion of a transport.

On arrival at Auschwitz . . . the rest is known. No one came back.

SHEMA YISRAEL, ADONAÏ ELOHENOU, ADONAÏ EHAD!

The Liberation

I thought I would be able to rebuild my life once my torturers had left the country. I'd been waiting for this day with an overpowering longing. I was straining towards it already on the day when the Germans pushed me like a mangy cur into a narrow cell in 42 Velissariou Street in Salonica.

The brutes had flattened my nose with their fists, kicked me in the kidneys and stamped on me with their boots.

Flat on my back on the floor of this small dark hole, I was breathing with difficulty. My nose was swollen and still bleeding. Holding my poor hurting head, I closed my eyes and gave rein to my thoughts in the darkness. Darkness and silence were my only safeguards; I could trust them with my misery.

I passed a restless night, dreaming that my two children were by my side. They too were in pain: they too had been beaten, poor little fellows. They were whimpering.

'Daddy, Daddy, what did we do to deserve this punishment? We haven't hurt anyone. Is it because we are Jews?' they asked. 'Are Jews always wrong?'

I looked at them blankly, but my thoughts were racing as I asked myself: 'Are these beatings going to alter my blood, my race?'

After holding me for two days, they let me go, turfing me out with a few extra clouts for good measure.

I found myself in the street. The sun was shining, too brightly for my comfort, my eyes had grown used to the dark. I pulled my clothes straight and centred the knot of my tie. Then suddenly I put my hand up to my face and used my handkerchief in an attempt to hide the blue marks that must be circling my eyes. Next my hand felt instinctively for the yellow badge, 'the sign that every Salonican Jew must wear sewn on the left-hand side at the level of the heart'.

Today I was as downhearted and despondent as could be.

A bootblack offered to polish my shoes. I envied this scapegrace. He was Aryan and free. He wore no yellow badge. He was more fortunate than my kids. His life was not at risk. The bootblack was of lordly race, the same race as the Germans.

The longing to embrace my wife and hold my children tight lifted my spirits. Hope put heart into me, good times would come again and I'd rebuild my life. One day the Germans would be gone. The devil take them, I was going to rebuild my life!

I made it to the mountains together with all I had: my wife and my children. I made myself useful in minor ways while I was there, although I left no greater mark than the general run of partisans. I wasn't, for example, involved in any important operations. I'm an accountant, and the pen is my only weapon. I'm not very fit either: my digestion plays me up frequently, especially when I'm under strain. And anyway my physique is that of an accountant.

Sometimes I ask myself what source I drew on for the determination, the courage, to stand up to the Germans, to reverse the roles and decide to kill my enemies or be killed.

It may be that the story of some patriot, some free man, had sown long since in the depths of my being a hidden strength. I remember when still very young being moved and excited by tales of sacrifices made for liberty. Perhaps these childhood memories gave birth to a miracle. I have a clear memory of uttering aloud one night the old proclamation: Liberty or Death!

Everyone in the house was asleep. I could hear the boots of the German patrol ringing on the pavement. Yes, that was the night when I took the decision to leave the ghetto and head for the mountains.

Certain rallying cries, heard a thousand times, can assume a sweep, particularly in moments of despair, that fills our whole horizon. Liberty or Death! is at once a commonplace and a powerful source of superhuman strength capable of taking on any opposition with the obstinacy born of despair. Liberty or Death! What magnificent words, fuelled as they are by the burning conviction that behind the darkest shadows light and liberty await us.

This was the light that visited me in my dark room that night. It shone on my children sleeping peacefully. It laid its finger on Sarah, whose gentle face, even when she slept, retained a look of suffering and fatigue. This soft light made no hero of me, no, yet it showed me the road that I must take with my wife and children. It lit my steps along the glorious avenue of liberty where a man can confront the most redoubtable of foes.

My wife and children followed me from one village to another. I would leave them in the company of the Resistance whenever I was sent on a mission by those in command. Sometimes we were parted for three, four, six weeks. They never complained; I had succeeded in convincing them that we were on the right path, the one that gave us the upper hand over the Germans.

At last the day of Liberation came: 30 October 1944. We came back to Salonica, the town we had been born in, to find my house occupied by others, my household goods vanished. I and my wife and children found shelter in an outbuilding in the yard of the Monastiriote synagogue.

Here in this yard, close to the house of God, we were free at last. Free to die in peace, if that were to be our fate.

Sarah fell ill as soon as we arrived. Each evening she was feverish; her face became red and congested, her eyes too bright. Next morning, in contrast, her temperature fell, and she was pale and listless. What effort it cost her on waking after a restless night to satisfy her two heedless lion cubs roaring for their breakfast.

In a matter of weeks I lost my beloved wife. Peacefully she breathed her last in a hospital bed.

When we were still in the mountains she was saying that she had reached the end of her strength. It was her faith in God's justice that kept her going; she always believed that victory would come. She wanted to die in her home town, among such of her own people as had survived.

That victory is yours, my beloved Sarah, you have attained eternal peace, which eludes us, alive and wretched as we are.

I had my wife buried in the stretch of unbuilt ground we call the new cemetery. She rests there next to four Jews who enjoy, like her, everlasting peace. They are freed from the wickedness of man. The earth is saturated with it.

The sacrifice of tens of millions of victims has not proved sufficient to bring peace on earth.

'I'll rebuild my life,' said I one day.

This I heard from a friend of mine, a commercial employee, a survivor.

IM

V

During your lifetime and during your days

Robert Matarasso

The pages of typescript left by Robert Matarasso at his death in 1982 represent the incomplete draft of a memoir begun, worked at with intensity over a period of a year or more and then left in abeyance at the tense point where the family were about to collect the precious Ausweis which would allow them to leave the ghetto and return to relative freedom. Although covering much the same ground, his account belongs to a different genre from his father's eye-witness report. Written 40 years after the events, it is an exercise in long-term memory. It is also an exploration by a man in middle life of the boy he once was, who had been forced to grow up far too fast and who bore lifelong the scars of what he had endured in those malleable years. In his very first sentence he puts this question, indirectly, to an imaginary reader: 'You may well ask me why I write.' He runs through the obvious answers without deciding, and finally offers this: 'I don't know, and it matters little. For in the presence of certain realities, reasons become almost impertinent.' It seems right to leave experience to speak for itself.

There are some things, though, that need to be said to facilitate understanding. Robert was his parents' only child, long awaited, at times perhaps despaired of, and he enjoyed, as he recognized, an indulged childhood:

Educational principles were vague in those days, and seemed to rely almost entirely on a lax discipline curbed only by the moral standards of the time. My upbringing followed the established pattern. No form of discipline was ever imposed upon me, but I knew and understood well my duties which I accepted ungrudgingly, because at no time had any undue demands been made on me.

201

With a father who was Jewish by birth, tradition and upbringing, but not markedly observant, and a French Catholic mother, who saw her first duty as being to her husband's family, and who never reneged on her Catholic faith but practised it privately on feast days rather than openly and regularly, Robert was born less with divided loyalties than with inbuilt uncertainties. Neither religion made any definitive claim on him while childhood lasted. He mentions accompanying his mother when she went to mass. No bar mitzvah took place, to my knowledge. He thought of himself always as French, and in his mind it was merely a matter of time before he claimed his birthright. Being French was his one stable source of identity; however, his right to French nationality would have to be claimed on French soil before he was 21. Hearing in 1940 on his father's treasured wireless the 'unbelievable' news of the fall of France left him deeply shaken.

At thirteen, I knew confusedly that my life was to change, and the fear I felt at this precise moment was of a different nature to anything I had ever experienced before. I continued my carefree adolescence normally enough, but I kept this new dimension buried within me, as if my secret was a superstitious guarantee that no harm would come to me provided no one knew I was afraid.

The discovery in 1941 that the Germans, and not only the Germans but his Greek school friends too, categorized him as Jewish, came as a further shock. It seems also to have been felt as a humiliation – strangely, given that all his known relations, including the cousins he played with as a child, and almost all his parents' social circle were Jews. He had unconsciously absorbed a sense of 'otherness', reinforced by what had percolated via the wireless, by conversation overheard, by street talk, in the wind . . . This sense of not belonging – exacerbated by fear and confirmed by the practice of establishing a distance (he kept the parish priest at arm's length too), until he effectually belonged nowhere – runs through this memoir like a leitmotiv. Even after 40 years, he clung to the safety of masks: no one in Robert's writing is given their true name, though family names have been restored here to avoid further confusion in an already complicated story.

He attended a Greek primary school, then moved to the French lycée when he was twelve. And, like all Jewish children of his social class, he grew up with three languages:

As a matter of course I too learned to speak the curiously adulterated brand of fifteenth-century Spanish which was passed down the generations, acknowledging the passage of time by adapting a Greek or Turkish word here and there, when no Spanish equivalent existed. Centuries later, when Western culture spread through the Eastern Mediterranean with the establishment of foreign schools, French and Italian were cheerfully accepted as the ultimate concession to the vanity of the prosperous. There is an intangible sadness at the thought of having been a silent witness to the brutal extinction of these spoken words. They had been nursed through five centuries, and it cannot have taken more than three months to silence them for ever.

After school, the streets were the playground in that 'eminently secure society'. There were plenty of friends; one in particular lived just opposite, on the upper floors of the house where Isaac Matarasso had his surgery. This boy's father, a civil servant and childhood friend of Isaac, had a son the same age as Robert. Andreas (a pseudonym) makes his entrance on the second page of Robert's story, and turns up regularly thereafter at every crux, like some not always well-intentioned sprite. We first meet him on 10 April 1941. The German army had occupied the city the day before, while the Greek troops regrouped on the farther side of the town in a desperate effort to stop them. There was fear abroad and in every house.

You Are a Jew

That afternoon, I crossed over to the surgery with my father. Sitting on the stairs, a grin on his narrow face, was Andreas Faretsos.

'Did you see them?' he asked in a low, excited voice.

'Yes, I saw them.'

'My father says that our troops are waiting for them on the Aliákmon river. We will stop them yet, you will see, Robert . . .' Then, as an afterthought: 'My father also said that the Germans hate Jews and that they will kill you all.'

I had often thought of this. I had heard my parents talking of the events of 1935 in Germany, of the Nuremberg laws and the plight of German Jews. It had meant little to me, except perhaps that over the years I came to regard the Germans as my own personal enemies. I now remembered that a few years ago, while on holiday with my parents in Yugoslavia, we had come across a little church in the island of Bled which possessed a wishing bell. Tradition had it that a wish would come true if one pulled three times on the rope while repeating the wish three times. In the prescribed manner I had three times wished Hitler dead.

'I am not a Jew,' I said at last. 'You know that.'

'Your father is,' retorted Andreas stubbornly, 'so you must be.'

I understood well this uncompromising logic. But I was hurt. I had been called a Jew before, of course, at school or in the street, but it had not seemed to matter very much then. Later that evening I wanted to ask my father questions that I knew I could hardly formulate, and for which, I also knew, my father would have no answers. So I remained silent, and when I fell asleep that night I was tired and very anxious.

The Wireless

A few weeks later the Occupying power started flexing its muscles with orders affecting only the Jewish community, the members of which were specifically identified by bloodlines.

•

My father was in conference. An informal affair, with three of his close friends sitting round the dining-room table, sipping a black mixture that smelt of coffee and tasted like beans. The first, Mr Barzilaï, was a serious man, a bachelor who had retired early and, having saved enough, lived comfortably in Salonica's most fashionable hotel, the Mediterranean, where he kept a permanent room. The other two were Alexander Faretsos, Andreas's father, and Gaspar Calvo, a member of the council of the Jewish community.[65] The last looked and was a frightened man. By the very nature of his position, he had twice, we knew, come into contact with the German authorities. Faretsos was an administrator in the Town Hall and a childhood friend of my father's. Their friendship had somehow drifted onto a more formal plane when Faretsos married late in life. It was murmured that his wife, the daughter of a village Orthodox priest, had resented her husband's friendship with a Jew. He was a small man, with large glasses, and almost bald. His position at the Town Hall gave him a special standing in the community. People approached him in the street seeking his help over some difficulty with an inefficient and self-satisfied administration: Alexander Faretsos was a fixer.

'I have received bad news, Isaac . . .', he started. There was little doubt that he meant bad news for the town's Jewry. 'I hope that you realize the risk I take in telling you this . . . .' He stopped and surveyed his friends as if to emphasize the risks involved. Then: 'I mean personal risks, you understand, because the communication we have received from Dr Merten at the Town Hall is very clearly marked "Confidential".' He opened his paper as if to prove something, but it was only a scrap of paper on which he had inscribed a few cryptic words, which he turned back for us into an edict concerning the Jewish community.

First came the announcement of the imminent arrival of the SS representatives of the Commission for Jewish Affairs and the implementation of the Nuremberg race laws which would follow. In the meantime all Jews were to surrender their wireless sets, and a list of residential accommodation suitable for billeting German personnel was to be supplied. For the guidance of the Greek administration: was to be considered of Jewish race any individual with one or more Jewish great-grandparents, the present religious persuasion to be considered immaterial to this classification.

As Alexander unfolded his news, the three men appeared to slump in their chairs. I looked at my father. His face was longer than usual, very pale, with two deep lines that I had never noticed before, running from his nose to the corners of his mouth. Then, all at once it seemed, they started questioning Alexander.

Isaac Matarasso, Toulouse, c. 1912.

Andrée Matarasso, c. 1920.

Isaac Matarasso with his mother and sisters. Studio portrait taken during Tamar's visit to Toulouse to see Isaac, late 1917 or early 1918.

From left to right: Esther, Nelly, Isaac and Tamar. The mother and girls all died on the return trip to Salonica, when their ship was sunk by a submarine.

Andrée and Robert, Salonica, 1927.

The Matarasso family, Salonica, 1928.

Standing (from left): Albert, Rachel, unknown, Andrée; seated: Isaac (holding Robert), Lucie, Aaron, Alice, Haim, David; children: Ninon, unknown, Sam Benrubi, Maurice.

Isaac and Robert, 1931.

Robert, c. 1946.

Isaac and Robert,
Paris, c. 1951.

Robert and Pauline
Matarasso, Paris, c. 1951.

Aaron Matarasso's surviving children, Paris, early 1950s.

From left: Isaac, Albert, Alice and David.

Athens, 1956. Press photo taken to accompany an article recording the award of the Prix Desportes to Isaac Matarasso by the Académie de Médecine in Paris.

Isaac and Pascale Matarasso, France, 1955. The first grandchild.

Isaac Matarasso, Athens, 1957.
The last photograph.

Robert Matarasso,
England, c. 1976.

German troops man an observation post overlooking Salonica harbour, 1941.

A German corporal *(Obergefreiter)* leads three Jewish men in forced calisthenics on Eleftheria (Freedom) Square in Salonica, 11 July 1942.

German troops strolling on the waterfront near the White Tower, Salonica, c. 1941.

German forces destroy the port during their retreat, November 1944.

I withdrew to the window feeling slightly sick. I wanted some fresh air, but dared not open the window. I remembered only the last paragraph of the order: 'to be considered of Jewish race . . .' Then, I must be a Jew and Andreas had been right after all. But how could he have known? My understanding of the facts as I knew them became blurred with the new interpretation of the same facts as explained by Faretsos. My father was by my side, his arm round my shoulders. The others were still talking in low voices at the table. He drew me closer: 'Don't worry, Robert. Except for the wireless set which we shall have to give up, there is nothing in those orders which need concern us.' I felt the strength of my father's arm around me, and like the little boy I still was, I huddled quietly against him. I was aware that he was talking to me, but I did not want to understand the words he was saying, perhaps because I knew that my father was deliberately lying to me. But I accepted his gentle comfort because I had nothing else to cling on to.

That evening, my father took me out for a stroll. We walked the short distance to the sea front. In better days, the wide pavement along the sea was Salonica's rendezvous. Crowds walked up and down the promenade, from the little garden surrounding the White Tower to the Mediterranean Hotel, at the other end, a walk of a mile or so.

'You must not worry any more, Robert,' my father said at last, answering a silent question. 'These are difficult times and everything has changed so very much in the past months. What used to be right or wrong yesterday does not matter any more . . . Not for a while, anyway.' Very patiently and very deliberately my father unravelled for me the intricacies of our situation, guiding me into circumstances I had never suspected before, explaining the Germans' blind hate of anything Jewish, counterbalancing our bleak prospects with historical parallels, showing the futility of such undertakings. He skilfully blended the possible dangers to come with his unshakable belief in Germany's defeat. He led me through the pattern of our future lives, demonstrating that, in a concerted effort, we would have to learn to live cautiously in order to avoid the pitfalls of our uncertain existence. A sort of family balancing act, like walking on a tightrope. And in the end, incredible as it may seem, he made the whole thing appear manageable and somehow within my grasp, instilling at times the faintest sense of adventure in my thoughts.

We walked back in silence along the deserted street. Maybe my father thought that he had said all there was to be said. But he was wrong: he could not have foreseen what would soon become public knowledge. The 'final solution' of the Jewish problem had yet to be implemented by the Germans, although under the mantle of absolute secrecy plans to that effect were to hand in Berlin. Mr Barzilaï had talked of a policy of 'resettlement' of European Jewry in specially designated areas of Poland, but no one had given credence to such absurd notions, in spite of the fact that his source of information was an old and trusted friend in Berlin. For the moment I was only trying to come to terms with the situation explained by my father. I was calm and thankful to him for entrusting me with his thoughts and his fears, as if we were equals.

The following day, my father visited Alexander Faretsos, and when he returned, he was pale and very angry. He had asked his friend to keep his precious wireless for a while, and said that he would surrender instead an old set which stood unused in the backroom of the surgery. Alexander had flatly refused to become implicated. For some time, it appears, my father had pleaded with him, not for the sake of the set but simply because he needed the reassurance of his friendship. He did not prevail upon Faretsos, whose fear was real. My father had been wrong in his expectations, because he had forgotten that there are times when friendships should not be tested.

The Tram

Danger occasionally took on a more immediately threatening guise. Public transport in Salonica consisted of trams, and the Matarassos, with no car, will have used them regularly until, in February 1943, they became a privilege forbidden to Jews. Robert, like most boys, liked to think of himself as streetwise, but there came a day when he owed his life to the basic human feeling of a very ordinary policeman interpreting his duty in a way that could have cost him dearly. The German security police, or Schupos, were no doubt looking for hostages, or for civilians to shoot in reprisal for some infringement of regulations.

It was on a sunny July afternoon in 1942 that I underwent my first experience of imminent physical danger. The crowded tram in which I was riding was abruptly brought to a halt. From where I stood on the back platform I saw a row of German lorries parked along the pavement. Two long whistle blasts pierced the air, and I heard the uneven, thumping steps of men running heavily along the tramlines, shouting guttural commands. They came into w, implacable in their black boots and round helmets, 's held high across their chests, their sheathed bayonets 'ling merrily from their belts as they ran. When they ed to form a line along the cars, their backs to the , they had effectively sealed off all escape routes from the stationary tram. 'Schupos', I thought, recognizing the uniforms of the Schutzpolizei. I drew back from the exit door trying to hide behind the panicking passengers. My back touched the half-gate on the opposite side of the platform which opened onto the tramlines. There were no Germans there, only a few Greek policemen spaced out along the middle of the street, facing the tram cars. One of them, a fat little man, sweating in a uniform too small for him, was standing directly opposite the gate. The Schupos were boarding the car at the far end, and amid angry and familiar shouts of '. . .'raus . . . schnell . . ', were forcing the passengers towards the other exit, where I stood.

'Essi, éla, pidixé!' – 'You there, come on, jump!' – came a loud voice. I looked up, heart pounding in my throat. The fat policeman was looking straight at me. Beckoning calmly, he said in a rough voice: 'Jump, you fool . . . Jump, you're too young to die.' This time I pulled open the gate and jumped quickly, still hesitating to cross the street. 'Tréxé, paidi mou, Tréxé!' 'Run, lad, run . . . !' As I passed him, I heard him swear contemptuously at the Germans: 'Kératadés! Poustidés!' Another Greek policeman looked up briefly and turned away uninterested. I had already reached the pavement on the other side of the street. I kept running, out of breath, all my being concentrated on my shoulder blades. But there was no danger, and no one chased me. The Schupos were only interested in the passengers on the tram. Three hundred yards away, life went on as usual, the mass abduction passing unnoticed.

I sought refuge in a café and sat at a table out of sight. My hands were unsteady as I drank the cold, fizzy lemonade. Once again I felt the strange reaction of blind anger, and in my arrogance discounted the fat policeman's help.

'Kératadés!' I kept repeating softly to myself. A little later, I went out and retraced my steps to the corner of the street. The tram and the lorries had gone. There was no trace of the round-up, other than a small group who had witnessed the incident from the door of a grocer's shop and were now talking in low voices – the only epitaph for the hundred people taken off a tram that morning.

I walked slowly away and into the sunbathed stillness of a side-street, becoming gradually aware that I was cold and frightened and that there was nothing I could do to check the mounting wave of panic. The events of the past hour were sinking in, and I realized the extent of my vulnerability and how near I had come to being sucked away in a whirlwind of destruction. I stopped short, and the details of the tram episode became sharper in my mind till I could almost smell the mixture of alien tobacco and boot polish of the German police. Then, in a sort of eerie dream, I saw again the unshaven round face of the fat policeman whose stained tunic bulged under the armpits. Unable to focus properly, I felt my stomach tighten. My legs sagged under me. I turned towards the wall and vomited.

Meeting Wisliceny

The streets continued to provide the two growing boys with occasions for amusement and, increasingly, fear. We have a rough date for the following incident, as the two Gestapo officers in question only arrived in Salonica on 6 February 1943, three days after Robert's 16th birthday. Dieter Wisliceny and Alois Brunner were specifically sent to the city by Adolf Eichmann to organize the deportation of the Jewish community to Auschwitz–Birkenau. Wisliceny, who had already rid Slovakia of its Jews, arrived well informed and ready to act: the first communiqué announcing the establishment of a ghetto was issued on the day of his arrival, followed a week later by a second, imposing a number of restrictive conditions, including the wearing of the yellow star. In the following incident Robert is wandering around with no distinctive sign on his clothing, so it probably occurred before mid-February 1943.

•

I had seen SS men before. The 'Das Reich' division had been stationed in Salonica for a while, but that elite unit wore the field-grey uniform of the Wehrmacht, and there was little to distinguish them from the ordinary troops.[66] It was after Christmas that Andreas and I set eyes for the first time on the black uniforms of the SD. We had been idly watching the unloading of sacks of flour from a fishing boat moored on the mole when four SD officers emerged from the nearby Mediterranean Hotel. They stopped in front of the large revolving doors, and I noticed that they acknowledged the salute of passing officers by raising their arms in a tired Nazi salute. There was something inexplicably different about these men. Sensing the novelty, we sat casually on the parapet, surveying the officers. A few yards across the street, the little group continued their conversation, listening to one of them, a tall, heavily built man who appeared to be the ranking officer.

'Who are they, do you think?' I asked, observing the scene.

'I don't know. Maybe Gestapo. My father said they were in town. Let's go, Robert,' said Andreas suddenly. I didn't reply. I looked on, unable to lower my eyes.

'Come on,' insisted Andreas as he saw the big man strolling casually towards us, followed by the others. My heart started pounding. 'Robert . . .,' I heard Andreas pleading. But the Germans had no interest in us. They stopped short of the parapet, observing the dockers running up and down a narrow plank, carrying effortlessly the sacks on their backs and stacking them neatly on shore. Their heads and shoulders were covered with a film of flour dust and they worked incredibly fast, avoiding each other with precision as they met in the middle of the plank. I pretended to look at the boat, then, shifting my position slightly, I felt compelled to watch the Germans again. They seemed immensely square in their black boots and matching breeches. The tall man produced a cigarette case from his breast pocket and passed it round; then, on a sudden impulse, he reached out and offered it to Andreas with an amused remark in German. Andreas turned very pale and in a small voice I did not recognize said in Greek:

'No, Sir, Thank you, Sir, I don't smoke, Sir.'

'Liar,' I couldn't help thinking, retreating a few paces. There was a burst of laughter. The German, thinking the joke funny, was forcing a cigarette into Andreas's hands – 'No, Sir, No !' – and he started running along the seafront while I moved quickly away in the opposite direction, I could hear the loud laughter behind me, but I lacked the courage to look back. The next time I met Wisliceny, the tall, thick-set man would not be laughing any more.

The Break with Andreas

Preparations are under way for the move to the ghetto, which must be effected by 25 February 1943 at the latest. The break with Andreas was the first major change it brought about for Robert, but the relationship was already doomed. Each boy was being manipulated by hidden forces, and neither had the understanding, or probably the capacity, to resist. The friendship was of its time and place; they would have grown out of it anyway, but the manner of its ending left a scar, still evident in an unexplained reference to the 'Faretsos family' at a critical juncture in the family story later that year, in handwritten notes made by Robert 40 years later.

•

My father and I had been working in the surgery all morning disconnecting a piece of medical equipment. The machine was now packed in the same crate in which it had arrived from France some years ago, still bearing the original labels. My father took out of a drawer a small parcel, from which he extracted two identity cards and four bright yellow stars, saying softly: 'One for your jacket and one for your overcoat . . . Your mother will sew them on presently.'

I picked up one at random, and, holding it against my heart, I turned to the mirror over the washbasin. I had seen pictures of people wearing them, and though I had thought of little else in the past days, I didn't really mind.

'When are we moving?' I asked my father, who was sitting on the edge of his desk, looking at the loose pipes and disconnected wires on the floor. He had not been well of late. He was drawn and seemed tired.

'Oh, soon now, I expect. I have already sent some of our things to Dr Amariglio's house. But there is still all this . . .' His hand made a vague gesture.

I liked the idea of moving. We were to stay with the Amariglios. He was a doctor friend of my father's, and they lived in the restricted area. Then there was Rachel, Dr Amariglio's eldest daughter. No, I didn't mind moving, and the thought of Rachel dispelled all the traces of uneasiness I had felt.

'I will go and see Andreas,' I said, picking up my stars, and, leaving my father still sitting on the desk, I ran up the wide marble staircase. I met Andreas on the first landing, and we sat down as usual on the stairs side by side. Then I produced the yellow star, not knowing what to expect. Andreas examined it with keen interest.

'So you are a Jew then,' he said.

'I suppose I am, but so would you be if one of your great-great-grandparents had been one.' I had deliberately added an extra 'great', hoping to confuse Andreas or even sow a niggling doubt in his mind.

'Don't talk like that.' Andreas was cross.

'Does it matter, anyway?'

'I don't know . . . It doesn't matter to me – that you are a Jew, I mean. My mother thinks it matters, though.' He couldn't resist, and tried the star on his lapel, as though it were a flower.

'Not like that, you silly, on the heart,' I said laughing, and I clapped the star on Andreas's chest with my open palm. He tried to tear if off, and I fought back to keep it there, still laughing.

'Get away from me, dirty Jew!'

I stopped tussling. Still holding the star on my friend's chest, I asked:

'Will you come and visit me in the new house?'

'Yes, of course I'll come. But my mother won't like it. She doesn't want people to see me in the street with you wearing that star. She always says that Jews are bad luck.'

It was then that I knew that Andreas would never visit me, but I did not try to find out why he was lying. His cheeks had turned pink, and somehow I was glad that he would never come, although I felt dispirited that Andreas had suddenly so little place in my life.

'Come on,' I said more cheerfully, 'I've got to have some photographs taken. You coming?'

'No, I'm going home. I've got things to do.' He didn't look back as he climbed the stairs. I didn't know that I wouldn't see Andreas again until the end of the war.

Leaving Tsimiski Street

Three days later the family moved out of their pleasant flat looking onto Tsimiski Street, a wide tree-lined boulevard with shops and cafés a short walk from the seafront. For Robert, though he didn't realize it at the time, it was the end of a very sheltered childhood. Dangers had been lurking behind doors for some time now. In certain conversations they had even penetrated the living room. More than once they had stripped off their Boy's Own disguises and shown themselves openly in the streets. He might have been thought to have grown up in this interval, and in some respects, as he has shown us, he had. But the 16-year-old who, faced with leaving home for good, retreats briefly to his room, goes through what remains of his belongings and is relieved to find that his mother has packed his most cherished things, because the decisions would have been too much for him, is still a child. It is not surprising that his parents were insistent on getting him out of the house on this last stressful day, yet his inability to take the least responsibility must be attributed to an upbringing that had laid only childish duties on him.

•

It was a crisp day, and the street was busy. I left the house, for the last time in my life as it turned out, and walked the few yards to the crossroads, conscious of wearing the infamous yellow star. I was standing looking idly at the passing traffic when I heard a voice calling me.

'Eh, Robert . . . Come here . . .' I saw fat Mr Berberian beckoning from the door of the delicatessen which he ran with his brother, a little man as thin as he was fat. Laurel & Hardy they had been nicknamed in the neighbourhood. They had known me since childhood. My mother shopped there, and my father bought his Dutch tobacco from the cigar counter.

'Do you want to work the "Sefilt"?' he asked me with a broad grin. The 'Sefilt' was a machine, a huge coffee grinder standing at the back of the shop, its large copper hopper gleaming against the whitewashed wall: a monstrous black machine, built by a Mr Waterhouse in Sheffield at the turn of the century. A wide belt emerged from the ceiling above and ran round the black ribbed wheel tastefully decorated with bright red flowers. The solid polished-oak container that collected the ground coffee stood high on a black metal frame embellished with the same delicate design. The machine was known to all as the 'Sefilt', and no one had ever challenged Mr Berberian's pronunciation [of Sheffield]. His coffee grinder had stood idle for months for lack of coffee beans. So, for his pleasure, and to demonstrate that he was still in business, Mr Berberian started his machine for a few minutes every day, dimming the neighbourhood's lights in the process. The noise, combined with the aroma that the Sefilt seemed able to exude, even when running empty, attracted sometimes a passing customer. It was then that Mr Berberian rose to unsuspected heights. With the customer cornered between the machine and his own massive bulk, Mr Berberian explained that he was expecting a large consignment of Brazilian coffee beans. The machine had to be prepared. Of course, he would let his customer know when he received his delivery. Better still, he would put aside for him a large bag of freshly ground coffee. But in the meantime, would he be interested in two tins of the best German ersatz coffee to be found in town? He had kept the tins for a very special customer ... Yes, Mr Berberian was still in business, and had never ceased to be since he had drifted to Salonica from his native Armenia, a refugee from the massacre of his people by the Turks.

The shop was empty. Mr Berberian took me behind the till and pointed at the contact switch on the wall. I pushed the ebony handle and the 'Sefilt' shuddered into life, an irritating noise of metal grinding against metal filling the shop.

'This is a special favour, you know. I don't allow anybody to touch this machine,' shouted Mr Berberian, rubbing the copper with his handkerchief. 'As you are going soon now, I thought maybe you would like to work the "Sefilt".' He had turned his back to me and was fiddling with the controls. Without turning, he handed me a sesame seed cake, sticky with syrup and then switched off the machine.

'Bad people these Germans,' he said and spat his disgust, 'but they will never do to you what the Turks did to us Armenians.' His face contracted with memories: 'I was a boy then, but I remember ... I remember well. You are lucky, because your father is an important man. My father was a shepherd. But you will remember all the same. When everything is normal again,' he said looking at his empty shelves, 'when everything is normal again, you will remember that "kokarda", that yellow star that they have pinned on you. And it is good that you don't forget. Never. When are you leaving?'

'Today, this evening, Mr Berberian'. The fat man sensed the uncertainty in my voice. 'Do you want to help me? Have you time? I have much to do and my brother is away.' I wondered what it was that Mr Berberian had to do in his empty shop, but I accepted. I worked all morning, moving sacks of dried beans and barrels of salted fish in the storeroom. Mr Berberian came to see me between customers and kept giving me small sticky sesame cakes which made me thirsty. I wanted to go now. I thanked Mr Berberian, who seemed to want to say something, but he changed his mind and went back into his storeroom and closed the door firmly behind him.

It was still early when, quite unintentionally, I found myself in the little garden surrounding the White Tower. I avoided a group of children playing under a solitary swing, and sat on a bench, unnoticed. I kept my left hand pressed against my chin, and in an attempt to hide the yellow star pinned on my chest I stooped forward. Concealing my identity was becoming an obsession, and one that greatly embarrassed me. When I walked in the street I skirted the walls, my right shoulder projecting forward, my left arm half folded against my chest. I was resentful and profoundly ashamed to be seen wearing the star, although I knew that there was nothing in the world I could do about it.

For a time I sat almost motionless and, becoming increasingly bored, I looked up at the deserted café which stood at the end of the garden, its front door boarded up for the winter, its flower beds overgrown and desolate. In the summer, I knew, the little café would stir into life, there would be music and song, and couples would dance the night out under the canopy of multi-coloured bulbs strung over the dance floor. In the summer . . .

The thought of the long walk across the esplanade made me uneasy because I could devise no practical means of hiding my star in the open space. I need not have worried though. When I eventually left the garden, the esplanade was almost deserted, and it was only as I approached Dr Amariglio's house that I saw small groups of men, women and children walking in the same direction. I overtook them easily enough at first, but then my progress was hampered by more people, who seemed to appear in front of me at each street comer. It was only then that I realized that all these people were Jews, who like myself were entering the restricted area. Soon I was slowed down to a crawl, so unbearably slow that when I recognized Dr Amariglio's in the distance, it felt as if time itself was standing still and it took me an age to reach the steps of the house. There I paused and surveyed the extraordinary procession. They were an odd assortment of people of all ages and all walks of life. They were carrying suitcases and parcels, and as they walked out of step towards me, a multitude of yellow dots moved slowly up and down, undulating like strings of Chinese lanterns, and inducing in me a kind of soporific spell.

At first I saw nothing else. Yet gradually I became conscious of a mood of extraordinary submissiveness, which seemed to bind them together as if in prayer. They were silent and composed, and their resignation professed their allegiance to an intractable God who demanded so much and to whom they submitted with the prophetic resignation of the chosen. Through generations of undisturbed existence their sense of impending adversity had never been eroded: persecution was the ultimate condition of their existence. Today the last component of their lives had fallen into place and there was no more to be said.

I watched them passing for a long time, feeling part of them and yet so distant, and when I knew that they would tell me no more, I turned away and knocked at the door.

Between Fear and Hope

Robert acknowledges that his recollection of the next three weeks – it can hardly have been much more – was extremely patchy. The Amariglios had four children. He had been looking forward to renewing his acquaintance with Rachel, the eldest, and these two at once lost themselves in an adolescent crush, sitting hour after hour on the low wall bordering the terrace. 'I lived,' he writes, 'oblivious of the events in the streets of the ghetto.' He seems to have been oblivious too of the overcrowding in the house – described in such detail in his father's account – and of the existence of Rachel's three siblings, who must have been constantly underfoot making their own demands for care and attention. In Robert's memory the house, where his father saw only sadness and pandemonium, was 'a haven of normality'. Yet out of this pearlescent mist certain scenes stand out with exceptional clarity. Fear and curiosity were usually the drivers: he admits to the anxiety aroused in him each evening by the hours of talk between the adults round the kitchen table, and going upstairs to lie awake in bed. Until, on 14 March, fate rearranged the cards.[67]

•

One morning, shortly after the closure of the ghetto, I noticed my parents sifting through the documents that, several months earlier, Father Katz had given to my mother.[68] They were both sitting at the kitchen table, bent over the papers, looking old. I overheard bits of their conversation.

'We must try, Andrée. If it is true, we must try.'

'Do you think it is? Are you sure?'

'No, I am not sure.'

I was intrigued and stepped into the kitchen.

'. . . Come in, Robert, come in and shut the door. Do you remember the Walbergs?' he asked me without warning. I searched my mind and remembered Kyria Poppi, a buxom dark-haired and very beautiful woman, and her thin and ailing husband, who spoke Greek with an appalling accent.

I also remembered all the gossip about them. He had arrived in Salonica from Russia soon after the October Revolution, a destitute and sick man. A Jew who had backed Kerensky and whose luck had run out.

She was a sensuous woman who, before her marriage, had been a dancer at the notorious and only nightclub in town, a Christian girl whose origins were as obscure as her indiscretions were flagrant.

'Well, Robert, you and I are going to pay a visit to the Walbergs.'[69]

I was astounded and looked at my parents questioningly. But neither of them explained. Presently I asked my father and he replied in an odd impersonal voice: 'I heard yesterday that there is a regulation, a kind of exemption in the law if you like, which may concern us. You, your mother and me, and of course all the others who are married to Christians. It seems that we may be permitted to leave the ghetto . . . and perhaps there will be no need to wear this any more,' he added pointing to the star on his jacket.

I remained silent and, taken aback, I began to shake.

'Here, sit down. I will explain.' But he didn't, and instead went on: 'I heard that the Walbergs will be leaving the ghetto today, and that Poppi has obtained some sort of document from the Kommandantur, where she knows . . . well, people . . .' My father stopped again, unwilling to explain what was common knowledge, that Poppi had been seen in the company of German officers so often that her reputation had not gone unscathed.

'So I want to hear from her if there is any truth in this rumour.'

He put the emphasis on the last word, trying to contain our hopes. But he still did not explain why he wanted me to go with him.

An hour later we were on our way through the crowded streets of the ghetto. My father stopped and knocked at the door of a house that was close to the SD headquarters, and from where we stood I could see no. 42 and the German security police guarding its entrance.

Mr Walberg opened the door and did not appear surprised to see us. He led us through the entrance hall and when we entered the living room, we found Poppi sitting next to a gramophone, a stack of records balanced on her knees. In front of her was one of those Turkish brass coffee trays on short wooden legs, and in it was an ashtray full of cigarette ends. Poppi was wearing a tight-fitting dress that moulded her body admirably. Her long dark hair was combed back without a parting, and her air of assurance was disconcerting. She looked up and immediately jumped to her feet, a broad smile on her face, her head slightly to one side, provocative as she approached, because this was her style.

'Dear Dr Matarasso,' her voice was deep and disturbing. 'Come in, come in, please . . . Vladimir,' she ordered her husband, 'Dr Matarasso will have a coffee.' And without waiting for my father to answer: 'Is this your boy, Doctor? What a good-looking lad,' she said, running her fingers through my hair. I smelled her body close to mine and felt her moist palm on my head, and I laughed with great embarrassment.

'Here, Dr Matarasso, come and sit by me.' She sat down again, crossing her legs high and leaning back, as immodest as ever.

I was left standing in the middle of the room, very conscious that I wanted to leave. Mr Walberg brought in the coffee with a glass of water for my father. He did not look at his wife as he put the tray in front of him, but said in his broken accent:

' Yes, it is true, Dr Matarasso. I will leave the ghetto today. I am a lucky man, you see . . . My dear wife got me this paper from her friends at the Kommandantur.' He handed a folded document to my father, then moved to the window and sat down, showing no further interest. I thought I heard Poppi spitting a swear word, but by then I was so embarrassed that I was pretending to look at a picture on the wall.

I did not hear what was said at the other end of the room, but Poppi's raucous, vulgar laughter dominated the conversation, which went on for quite a while. When my father got up, he was smiling and I heard Poppi murmur:

'For you Doctor, I would do anything, you know that . . . Yes, I will speak to Max. I will speak to him tonight. He won't mind since it is the law now . . . and anyway, Max will not refuse me anything, you know,' she added with a shameless smile full of insinuations.

My father seemed relieved, but he was ill at ease and flushed, and as he made no pretence of leaving, I assumed that he felt in duty bound to talk to Vladimir, who, standing by the window, was still sulking.

The two men exchanged a few words and inevitably talked of the future, but they had no interest in each other. Vladimir Walberg lived apart, in a world of small particulars he had laboriously carved out for himself in a foreign land and which contained much real pain. It was a short and uncomfortable conversation, and we left soon after in a mood of great anticipation.

The rest of the day must have been typical of many other days because I have no recollection of it until the evening, when the conversation revolved exclusively around what Dr Joseph, as I had come to call him, described as 'the miraculous developments of the day', which eclipsed everything else.

It was only later in the evening that the difficulty of obtaining the much-coveted document came home to us. The Kommandantur was situated outside the ghetto, and my father was not permitted to leave the restricted area. This, I remember, was a grave preoccupation and we searched in vain until, among irrelevances and repetitions, we stumbled on the notion of a go-between as the indispensable means of achieving our aim. A lesser man than Dr Joseph might have felt inclined to dissociate himself from a situation which at best was not his concern, and at worst made his own predicament more acute. But it was he who in his soft-spoken manner put substance into the dream when he uttered gently a single name:

'I think that Father Katz might help you, Isaac.'

And so it was that Father Katz came to see us the next afternoon. He was still with us when we heard the first rumours of the deportation, which had taken place early that morning in the suburb of Baron Hirsch. And when, like a blow falling on a bruise, came the news that the sick, the old and the orphans had also been taken away, I instantly knew what this meant, although no one had mentioned my grandfather by name.

I thought that my father was about to faint, so grey was his face, when he took his handkerchief from his breast pocket and pressed it against his lips and I watched my mother break into tears, so quietly that no one noticed her. The priest murmured something in Latin, and perhaps because he thought that I did not understand the implication of the news, he asked me to make some coffee. I had no wish to stay, and I knew that I did not want to be talked to. I walked out of the room and opened the garden door. A great stillness enveloped me as I sat on the low wall by the garden steps, drained of all strength and holding back the tears that filled my eyes. But I was unable to think or even to understand what the news really meant until, in shifting my position, I must have frightened a sparrow, because out of the stillness came a flutter of wings and with it, the first sign of returning reality.

Father Katz was standing by me: 'I've left your parents on their own. Please don't disturb them for a while.'

I could not tell him that I had no intention of going back into the house because I could not bear the sight of their distress.

'But later, tell your mother that I shall be returning tomorrow.' He was in two minds about telling me more.

'We have to go on an errand together, you know. To the Kommandantur. We should not be too long, I hope, but it is important that we go tomorrow, without fail.'

He was plainly worried about the impending visit, and he sat with me in silence. Then, quite unexpectedly, he asked me: 'How would you like to serve at Mass for me?'

The idea seemed so incongruous that I thought he intended saying Mass right now, in the garden. But he went on: 'You see, it is possible that tomorrow or the day after you may come to live at the mission for a while with your parents. Until we can find you a house, that is.'

'Why can't we go back home?'

He explained that our house had been requisitioned by the German army, and it was a long time before he convinced me that we could not return there.

'There is no other place except for the mission, Robert.' I visualized the long damp corridors of the mission house, adjacent to the church and surrounded by a grey wall capped with pieces of broken glass embedded in the cement as a deterrent to prowlers, the gravelled courtyard, overshadowed by tall, ageing trees, the grey metal gates which were never opened even when the bishop came from Athens for the confirmation ceremony. But I was grateful and I thanked the old priest, though maybe not as convincingly as I ought.

When at last Father Katz departed, the light was already failing in the garden and a sudden gust of wind made me shiver. I was experiencing a curious premonition of danger. The last few days had been unsettling, and I recognized the signs of a growing threat encroaching on my shrinking world. I saw danger everywhere: in Poppi's raucous laughter, in Vladimir's senseless bitterness, in my father's uncharacteristic reliance on the good will of a trollop. But it was not until I had witnessed my parents' uncontrollable grief that I became aware of the debilitating certainty of disaster and grew resentful at the awful recognition that my father was as frightened as I was. Then, quite unexpectedly, came to the fore the realization that I was on my own and I felt an immense sense of isolation. I think that it was then that I started tiptoeing out of my childhood.

The wind had dropped to a soft breeze when my father joined me in the garden. From the expression on his face I saw that he was calm again.

'Your mother has gone to bed,' he said. 'She was very tired but she will be all right tomorrow.'

I gave him Father Katz's message. He did not reply immediately. Then, as if trying to reassure me, he said: 'Tomorrow may bring good news.' But of my grandfather, to my relief, he said nothing.

The Prayer

From their individual viewpoints, both witnesses throw light on the faith and observance of the Jewish community in Salonica during the Occupation. I have listened too to the descendants of Aaron Matarasso; I think here of those of my generation who grew up in Greece. Already they saw their elders as 'relaxed' in their compliance with the religious laws. Increasingly felt to be outdated and irrelevant in the modern world, the religion of the ancestors remained respected as part of a revered tradition, with rites to be observed on special occasions. In this they were not unlike their Christian contemporaries, who merely found indifference easier, insofar as their religion was not an integral part of the history of their race. Isaac strikes me still as standing apart. In his outward behaviour he followed the mainstream. In the eyes of nieces and nephews he was agreeably modern and enlightened (Robert thought his father's fidelity to Jean Jaurès and Anatole France a bit old-fashioned) and certainly not 'religious', but in my memory – as in his writings – he was a man at peace with God, and open to His presence in whatever guise or metaphor He chose to reveal Himself.

His son, looking back at his 15-year-old self, startled to find his father one day 'unusually still' in his chair, wrote 40 years after the event, 'For a moment I thought that he had been praying, but then I knew that he would not know how.' Does the comment reflect an immaturity to be expected in an adolescent or a wider tendency to rest on the surface of a man so easy of approach, who made little of his many gifts, who loved the young and was the go-to 'uncle' of so many? The depths he kept to share with a few close friends can now be glimpsed by readers everywhere in the pieces written in memory of Mordoh Pitchon, Harbi Haïm Habib and Joseph Amariglio. It is not a historical past but a living tradition that is being celebrated here, and by a man who knows what he is celebrating: 'We were following the road trodden by millions of sons of Israel, singing the same song of grief and hope which lifted us out of ignominy into the sublime spheres of Jewish spirituality.'

And if, in this time of greatest trial, some of their leaders failed the people, their God was still with them. A few hours after the first deportation, a lone voice was heard proclaiming His presence in the Shema, and other voices were raised to join it. As I am not aware of any published description of that fleeting moment I give it here in RM's words. It is part of a longer and more distanced account of the first deportation, which carried his grandfather Aaron off to Auschwitz, and I cannot be certain that he was present to hear it in person. We have almost an hour-by-hour account of those two frenetic days when the dawn of hope for the Matarassos was horribly darkened within hours by the news from Baron Hirsch. However, the gathering crowd was only minutes away from the house in Sarantaporou Street, curiosity is in the nature of boys and Robert's interjection that it was 'an uncanny and disturbing experience' is a very personal turn of phrase – and an experience is surely defined by being felt. The adjectives too suggest an onlooker who belonged without belonging. The singing came and went, but the emotion it expressed was lasting.

•

It was not very long before the people of the ghetto learned of the devastation that had swept the suburb. The returning Jewish guards had families and friends, and the news spread quickly. The reaction was immediate. The people converged on the council offices. As they approached, they found themselves surrounded by Schupos, and the bulletin for the occasion was read by an agitated clerk: the resettlement had begun and the transportation of all the Jews to Poland was now official policy. Specific orders had been received from Berlin. The resettlement would continue until all the population had been transferred to Kraków. With that a list of 102 names of hostages was pinned to the door. Nothing would happen to them if the people kept their heads and obeyed orders, but at the first sign of disturbance the hostages would be shot. The trap had been sprung, and the people knew that their hour of trial was at hand. A stunned silence followed the announcement. Then, without warning, a slow incantation rose above the crowd, a lonely voice lost in a sea of heads was heard singing the psalm for the dead.

Others joined in, singing without expression. The lonely voice was faint and tired, but not a word was lost: *Shema Yisrael Adonai Eloheinu* . . . It was an uncanny and disturbing experience, an expression of faith and exclusiveness that lasted but a few moments. Slowly the crowd dispersed, passing through the ranks of the armed men, who were laughing. The Jews of Salonica had just lived their hour of collective defiance. There were to be no other forms of protest, no noisy demonstration, not even a public manifestation of grief. But the synagogue filled, a solemn vigil was kept, and it continued in full for the following 53 days.

VI

Listening to the witnesses

François Matarasso

'Whoever listens to a witness, becomes a witness.'
Elie Wiesel[70]

There were always stories. My earliest memories of Robert,
my father, are entangled with them. *Salonique* – we spoke only
in French – seemed ever close at hand, charmed from the air
by words alone. The city, whose streets he walked with his
parents, cousins and friends, where he knew and was known
by shopkeepers and café owners, to which he *belonged* in a
way that he never felt again, stayed with him throughout his
life. Though he never saw it after 1946 – *because* he never saw
it after 1946 – its sunlit ways glowed in his heart. He evoked
the White Tower on Salonica's waterfront so often, and with
such affection, that when I finally saw it, on a pilgrimage to my
father's birthplace after his death, it seemed to greet me like an
old friend. In this lovely, complicated city, so changed since his
1930s childhood and yet still so recognizable from his stories, I
walked with my father in spirit, alone, between the Aegean Sea
and the mountains of Macedonia. It was exactly 50 years since
the Liberation, half a century since the Germans had deported
nearly 50,000 of its citizens in fulfilment of a mad fantasy that
Salonica, and Europe, would be *Judenfrei*.[71] Historians still
calculate the effects of those years. Families still feel the loss.
On this jubilee I needed to be here, a *Mischling* like my father,
simply to affirm that they had not succeeded.[72] Not entirely.

•

There were always stories. When my mother cooked him
lentils, or kidney beans and rice, my father would talk about

the refectory that his grandfather had paid for so that poor Jewish school kids could get through the day with a hot meal inside them. He missed Greek food and brought supplies from his rare visits to Athens: tins of Kalamata olives, halva and red cod roe, from which I watched him make his own taramasalata, which we ate greedily with crusts of thick white bread. Such flavours were unobtainable in rural England in the early 1960s. When there were olives at lunch (usually because we were in France), Robert remembered his father eating *meze* with friends at a Salonican café table, and watching them compete to squirt the stones between thumb and forefinger as far as possible across the street. He showed us how to do it, but it was his embarrassment that made the story vivid to me. I didn't understand why he'd winced at such an innocent game, but I knew how uncomfortable it can be when your parents stand out in their difference.

Anything medical would inevitably bring up stories about his father. He set a match to cotton wool when I cut my hand. I watched it shrivel and turn from white to black, my hurt forgotten in fascination. He applied the calcinated remains to my finger, explaining that it would stop the bleeding, talking all the while about the simple lessons he'd taken from the doctor at home. I accepted my grandfather's authority and kindness in his son's love, familial transmission through words and touch. Cardboard pill boxes were still in use when I was young. Plain, white and round, their halves fitted snugly together so that the contents would not spill. Light as leaves, they were a delight to me, as they had been to him when he'd played with his father's stock while waiting for a consultation to finish. Isaac would take him sometimes when he made evening house calls. It's pleasant to walk in the cooling city: people are enjoying supper, ice cream or just taking the air. There is time to stop and talk.

Robert remembered accompanying his father to see patients in the poor neighbourhoods, where whole families lived in a single room or in shacks propped against the city walls. The atmosphere and the people were very different from the middle-class streets in which he walked to school and played with his cousins. The doctor didn't ask for payment from those in need. (Six and seven decades later, I met elderly people in Salonica and Athens who had been treated by *le docteur Matarasso* as children; gripping my hand, as if to connect physically with their past, they spoke fervently of his kindness.) But impecunious patients sometimes liked to present him with tokens of appreciation, and my father kept a curious object he called a 'nose flute'. Made from cheap grey metal, it had been given to him on one of these visits, but he never discovered the secret of extracting music from it.

He remembered too the man who gave the doctor a set of lock picks as a mark of esteem, and which were kept faithfully in a desk drawer, unused but respected. Robert, who never lost a certain youthful romanticism, was fascinated by such things. It was said that some Jewish families in Salonica still held on to the keys of houses in Spain they had been forced to abandon. Stories were the keys to unlock the doors of lost homes in another city.

•

Marika was part of that other city. He was a boatman who earned his bread rowing people and goods across the great bay that is Salonica's other half and a good part of its prosperity. Robert knew him as Marika, but it was actually the name of his boat. Customers hailed him from the quay by calling 'Marika!' and the identities of man and boat had fused with the passage of years. There are photos of him, presumably taken by Isaac in the late 1930s, that show a strong, thick-set man, sitting back on the rowing bench, big hands resting on his thighs. From the pocket of his shirt hangs a leather badge marked 436, the sign of his registered status. The camera has caught his lined face halfway to a smile, but he looks a bit unsure: there probably weren't many customers who wanted to take his portrait.

Another photo shows Robert, about ten years old, pulling at the oars, his face concentrated with effort under a white sun hat. Father and son regularly took exercise in this way. For a doctor of Isaac's time, physical training and fresh air were vital aspects of good health, as much part of modern medicine as antiseptics and vaccination. Robert cherished happy memories of rowing and swimming with his father, and he retained an admiration for a certain kind of masculinity that he associated with stoical toughness: John Wayne was a favourite. He told me that Isaac had once swum all the way round a British warship anchored in the bay of Salonica, earning the applause of the ratings on deck.

In Robert's childhood, and so in mine, Marika was a cheerful figure. He didn't tell me until years later, when I was an adult and he was (though no one knew it) in the last year of his own life, about his darker memories of the boatman. In the cold, hungry winter of 1942, with the shops empty and food rationed, Robert saw Marika shuffling along the streets by the waterfront, rifling bins and begging for food. His old army greatcoat, cut for a taller frame, dragged at his feet. People gave him what they could, an onion or a hunk of the damp maize bread they'd been reduced to, but it was not enough. One day Robert saw the old boatman fall to his knees and crumple to the pavement. He ran to help. Marika was on his side, knees drawn up to his chest. Robert saw dirt in his white stubble, and blood running from his nose. He tried to reassure the man, straightened his legs and raised him to a sitting position against a lamppost. A woman began to pray. Then a policeman arrived and shooed away the gathering crowd. My adolescent father walked home with his first knowledge of death. Forty years later, he wrote that he found it 'disturbingly acceptable'. There would be much more like this in the coming years.

•

Children are protected by the limits of their understanding. To the extent that my father spoke of the war, the Occupation and the Resistance, the events he recalled struck me as exciting rather than terrible. I lacked the knowledge to interpret them in any darker tones, and he was careful in his choice of tale and its telling. The Shredded Wheat on our breakfast table once prompted a story about British supplies dropped for the partisans who had rescued him from prison. There were, he said, boxes of Shredded Wheat, which the hungry soldiers mistook for *kadaif*, a favourite Balkan pastry made with filo threads, cheese, cream and nuts, and soaked in sweet syrup. They were disgusted by the dry, flavourless food and it was soon abandoned. Even then – I must have been seven or eight – the idea of sending cereals to the Resistance struck me as dubious, but I understood the story's underlying truths, about hiding, hunger and cross-cultural confusion.

I was mesmerized by the war, which cast unavoidable shadows across an otherwise sunlit childhood. I saw my father read avidly the historical accounts that were beginning to appear in paperback, as he sought to understand the pattern of events he had experienced as inexplicable and chaotic. He ignored Disney cartoons, taking me instead to see *The Longest Day* and *Battle of Britain*, dressed in jacket and tie for the occasion. My books and games were martial. Endless days were spent painting plastic soldiers and models of tanks and bombers. I sensed his interest, even approval, though he tried to talk me out of a preference for the more dramatic German versions, with their swastika transfers. But there was no serious connection between my toy guns and the twisted bullet that had missed him by inches and now dangled from his keychain. At school, our childhood game was called 'bang-bangs'.

In France, I accompanied him to ceremonies of remembrance and heard other stories of another Occupation, darker, and touching people I knew. In our village, a memorial recorded the names of the dead and deported. Everyone remembered. I assumed that war would return, one way or another, bringing with it the end of everything good, and that belief, only childish at first, stayed. I cannot say when I first learned of concentration camps or heard their notorious names. It was something I knew, seemingly without being told. I had read *The Diary of Anne Frank* and *One Day in the Life of Ivan Denisovich* in my early teens, Primo Levi a bit later. When we watched *Holocaust* together in 1978, it was familiar territory, and we were both unimpressed by its American TV style. My father had spoken about Dr Menasche, Isaac's friend and colleague from student days, and a gifted musician who'd taught him to play the flute. With his wife and teenage daughter, Albert Menasche was deported to Auschwitz on 1 June 1943; there the family was separated and he was assigned to a camp orchestra. The only survivor, he subsequently wrote that 'it was better to be a musician than a doctor'.[73] My father kept a copy of his old teacher's book with his own father's papers. Was I 15 or 16 when I first read my grandfather's typescript? I can't be sure, but I don't think it was a revelation. It made clearer what I had already understood.

•

Many survivors are quiet about their experiences, or speak only and privately with those who passed through the same gates. Their children have written about growing up in a strident silence, where absences fill rooms. Their accounts unfold like investigations, as they painstakingly fill the gaps left in their own lives by parental taciturnity. That was not my experience. There were always stories. It was only as I grew older, as I read and learned, as I thought about what I'd been told and listened to relatives and others of that generation, that I saw how selective those stories had been. The happy childhood memories, even the stories of time with partisans, were accurate, perfectly true to my father's lived experience, but they were also shaped by a natural storyteller, so that weight was given where it was sought, while other truths were left in shadow. There were large omissions, especially time in the ghetto and in prison. My father never described himself as a 'Holocaust survivor', and today, almost 40 years after his death, I find it difficult to write that phrase, concerned about what he would say. I don't think he'd like to see it, plainly in those terms, although he kept the document stating it until he died. As I reached adulthood, and he passed 50, we spoke more and more about the past. I needed answers, and he, I think, needed them too, although our questions were different. I was at an age where the facts seemed important. He, knowing them, sought their meaning, a quest I took up only in his absence.

Before then, in early adolescence, I had stumbled on a secret. Alone together on a long car journey – sitting on the front seat beside him as he drove with pleasure and assurance is an abiding memory – I had asked, as so often, about Salonica, the family and the war. As he spoke, a realization gradually came to me. 'So Oncle Haïm, Tante Alice, Oncle Sam – all the family in Greece is Jewish?' 'Yes,' he answered, 'but you must never tell anyone.'

I was shocked, not at learning that my Greek relatives were Jewish but at his injunction to keep it secret. It seemed to me absurd. What danger was there? I knew about the Shoah, albeit still in somewhat broad terms, but I believed in 'Never forget' and 'Never again'. I lived in a welfare state which had abolished the death penalty and made racial discrimination illegal. We were safe. I was safe. And I was safe (and ignorant too) because I was Catholic. The religious commitment my father had made in 1945 remained firm, and his children were brought up in the Catholic faith, educated by monks and nuns. But he had learned at an impressionable age how unsafe were such differences: they had extracted him briefly from the ghetto, but they had not saved him from arrest and imprisonment. It was only chance that had kept him from the trains that ferried his grandfather Aaron to his death, and with him the community in which he had been nurtured.

The secret I learned on that car journey was not that some of my family were Jewish but that my father was afraid, perhaps even ashamed, at the prospect of anyone finding out. My heart breaks at that idea, but in the long years since, as the witnesses have died and their memories have stiffened into history, where they can be taken for granted, forgotten, disdained, discredited and denied, I have learned something else. My father's fear was not misplaced. 'Never again' was never true, even then in the innocence of my youth, when wars of decolonization gouged bitter new divisions, when cold warriors carpet-bombed farmers with napalm, when apartheid and segregation were preached in the name of civilization, when cultural revolution devoured anyone who could be called bourgeois. 'Never again' was not true then. It is not true now. The victims and the perpetrators change: the crimes do not. My father's fear was not misplaced.

Perception is at the heart of this story. How we see ourselves, how others see us and we see them: how we treat each other in consequence. I had not seen my Greek family as Jewish because my references for Jewishness were East European. My relatives were French-speaking, secular and Mediterranean. Religion didn't come up: we sent Christmas cards to Greece and received, I now realize, New Year cards in return. The idea of a Catholic Holocaust survivor is disconcerting to some people. It crosses boundaries and defies assumptions; it raises questions. It is a *Mischling*. But even saying that is to follow, however unconsciously, the most stupid ideology of the twentieth century: it is to see as a 'race scientist' saw.

So my father's stories were not shared outside the family. They would require explanations whose terms could not be relied on. Cover might be blown. Being a French Catholic in 1960s rural England was odd enough. Acceptance must be worked for; it could be lost in a moment. Robert had learned it in 1941, when he discovered not that he was – in some people's eyes – a Jew, but that it mattered. No wonder he loved talking of the city where he had belonged. Nowhere could be like that again after he had seen its ruthless, methodical destruction.

•

My grandfather died in 1958, a few months before I was born. Even so, he was an important presence in my life, refracted through his son's memory and its river of stories. Later, he became a presence through his own words: the public ones addressed to his fellow Greeks, and the more private ones shared with family and friends in letters, notes and inscriptions. And he was reflected in the words of those who loved and admired him.

My father died in 1982. I was there; I shall never forget it. His absence has shaped my life as much as his presence did. My father's words were never public, and he wrote less than his father, but there were always stories, and they stay with you like nothing else.

In October 1994 I went to Greece for the first time, alone. In Athens, I saw Sam Benrubi, my father's cousin and contemporary, in whom I felt again that generous, open, Greek Jewish spirit that had defined my early life. We visited my grandparents' graves, marble tomb chests shaded by pines in the Jewish section of the city's third cemetery. And

I read the inscription with which Robert had said farewell to his mother:

Vivante tu nous as tout sacrifié
Morte, laisse-moi imiter ton exemple

Robert*

Andrée was always in the background when my father spoke of Salonica, supportive, enabling, but rarely an actor in events where Isaac seemed to hold his attention. Now I guessed something of her importance to him, and I regretted how little he had spoken of her. In that quiet cemetery, with Sam, I came as close to meeting my grandparents as has been given to me.

And then I flew to Salonica, so that there would be a Matarasso in the city on the 50th anniversary of its Liberation. I walked down Tsimiski Street, looking for 'a row of three-storey houses, neatly rendered in sandy stucco and embellished with white plaster cast mouldings of classical design', but the building in which my father had grown up was gone. Still, I could see where it had stood, and imagine him walking with his father the few blocks to the sea, where Marika might be waiting for customers. From the first-floor window of the Jewish community offices, where I had been welcomed by the Secretary, Albertos Nar, I watched the Ohi Day parade that commemorates Greece's rejection of Mussolini's 1940 ultimatum, and remembered my father seeing the first dust-caked tank and German motorcyclists rumbling down the same street in April 1941. Double vision comes easily to those who go, as I had done,

---

* 'In life, you sacrificed everything for us, in death, let me follow your example.'

to places they know intimately but at second hand, through talismanic tales passed from one generation to the next. In Salonica, I spanned the difference between the exile, who has belonged and can hope to go home, and the exile's child, who has never belonged at all, who must make a home out of stories. In recalling his last days in the Tsimiski Street flat, my father wrote:

> I felt comfortable among the familiar objects. The smell of the freshly ironed pillow case lingered in the air, pleasant. I felt a great surge of tenderness for my way of life, for everything I knew and was mine. My world was a tidy and easy-going world and I loved it.

Sam Benrubi tried to make me feel at home in Salonica. He made calls and opened doors, introducing me to people in the Jewish community. For the first time in my life, I met strangers who asked no explanation of my name or for some implied proof of legitimacy. My heritage was understood: it had a place. Among those who welcomed me was Rena Molho, who immediately invited me to come and see her when I phoned unannounced, cooked lunch and shared her immense historical knowledge of Jewish Salonica. In conversations with people who had known my family or who valued my grandfather's work, personal stories became public ones. They became part of a collective history, not just one family's origin myth. Knowledge I'd absorbed like milk to make my emotional skeleton was independently confirmed by other witnesses. Often they could add details, or explain things that had puzzled me. I understood why Isaac and Robert had been imprisoned in the Heptapyrgion, and how they could have escaped.[74] I walked streets that had, for a few months in 1943, been designated as ghettos, and heard about the life that my family had briefly shared with so many others there.

And then Rena Molho showed me the Jewish primary school. The oldest part is a small, neoclassical building with three tall, arched windows and stone balustrades, framed by pilasters, the principal floor supported by a rusticated basement. In a frieze below the parapet I could make out letters in Greek and Hebrew: *Matanoth Laevionim.* And high on the wall at one end was a long inscription on a marble plaque:

Hot Kitchen
By **Aaron Bohor Matarasso**
Who contributed to its construction
In memory of his dear departed wife
Tamar Aaron Matarasso
And his dear departed children
Nelly Aaron Matarasso
Esther Aaron Matarasso
Who disappeared tragically
On 13 January 1918
As well as of **Henri Alberto Matarasso**
On 3 August 1928
Give Bread to the Needy
Isaiah 58–7

Jacques Moshe
Engineer ETP[75]

Before this was a school, it was a kitchen for poor schoolchildren, the refectory that my father told me his grandfather had founded. It had survived, preserving the names of four murdered members of my family. Aaron had retired after his wife, Tamar, and his daughters, Nelly and Esther, had been killed when the ship on which they were returning to Salonica in 1918 was sunk by a German or Austrian submarine. He had devoted his energies to charity, principally Matanoth Laevionim, which had been founded in 1901, when a group of Jewish doctors had discovered that the epidemic of collapses by children in the city's poorest neighbourhoods was due to malnutrition, not disease. Over the years several refectories were established, and by 1940 they were feeding 2,580 young people each day, including 800 here at the Réfectoire Matarasso. I stood transfixed before this trace in stone of my great-grandfather's life. My father's stories were not just mine: they were part of a city's history, its fabric. Later, in one of the books given to me by Albertos Nar, I read this tribute to Aaron, written in 1948 by the then Chief Rabbi of Salonica, Michael Molho:

In 1941, [Matanoth Laevionim] was presided over by Aaron Matarasso, a good and simple man, whose life was largely dedicated to the public good, without show or vanity. Despite his very advanced years, this virtuous man was deported to Poland and sent to the crematorium when he stepped from the train in Birkenau.[76]

I stood and looked at the inscription, over the thick black bars that now protect the Jewish primary school. Fortunately, Rena Molho was at hand to explain to the security guard why I wanted a photograph.

•

There are always stories. It's how we make sense of our lives, constructing meaning by telling and retelling, selecting, omitting, refining, polishing. We are at home in language, Ladino, French, Greek, English, German. We reach out to one another with words, and in everyday life they are sufficient. We can understand and be understood, even if only in part, or in translation. But sometimes, more often than we like to believe, words fail us. Those who returned, like Leon Batis and Albert Menasche, feared that they would not, *could* not be believed. My father's flute teacher asked if his words would be seen 'only as the wanderings of a poor mind thrown off its course', because he knew that his story 'surpasses all human imagination'.[77] No wonder so many withdrew into silence, fearful of denial and fresh assault. There is more than one way to erase a person. The Nazi state, with its mastery of criminal euphemism, understood that history is not written by the victors alone. Its effort to eradicate Jewish life in Europe extended beyond people, buildings, graveyards, artefacts and culture, beyond its own sites of murder even, to poison the wells of language itself so that the stories could not be told or, if told, could not be understood. What, after all, is 'special treatment'? Even the fantasy of a 'final solution' is a linguistic sleight of hand.

I grew up believing the survivors' doubts understandable but misplaced. We were safe. Never forget; never again. I had listened to the stories, over and over. Repetition did not dull them for me: on the contrary, with the passage of time, increasing knowledge and maturity allowed them to speak to me in new ways, with more complexity and closer to the truth. Today I recognize the part played in that by personal connection. These were family stories, told me by my father, aunts, cousins. They spoke of what had happened *to them*, what they had seen and who they had heard. They were consistent in every respect, and they explained the life I had. They were stories, but they were true stories.

Bernhard Schlink, the jurist and writer, has written about the burden of the past that successive generations of Germans must carry.[78] So too, in one way or another, do those who suffered under the Nazi regime: European nations from France to Russia, Norway to Greece, and those targeted as particular enemies of the *Volk*: disabled people, gays, Roma and Sinti, socialists and, *primi inter pares*, Jews. There is no certain figure for the number of victims, nor any way to assess the continuing effects of this European trauma on descendants and successors. But I'm not sure what such calculations would add: we are where we are; we are who we are. Whatever our own connection with victims or perpetrators, bystanders or survivors, the moral task of all human beings is the same: to make good with the materials at hand.

But in recent years I see better the difference between those who are directly connected to this criminal past and those who are not. I see that there are many, indeed the great majority of people in the world, for whom the events described in these pages are just stories, things that happened to other people, far away and long ago. Or didn't. I have read the denials, the fantasies and the lies. The danger, in these confused, relativist, postmodern times, is to confuse fact with the meaning of fact. Truth may be complex and elusive, but it does exist. The Occupation of Salonica and the planned murder of its Jewish citizens took place, and was witnessed by people I knew. My grandfather took pains to record and document what happened as scrupulously as his training and position allowed, while he worked to alleviate its effects. He wrote truth to the very best of his capacity, for the dead and for the living. He wrote more personally about those he had known and lost – more personally, but with equal truth. My father's stories were told for other reasons: to keep alive, even in words, what had been lost, to understand and to pass on to his children what had mattered to him so much. Other reasons, but always truthful.

The meaning of what the witnesses report is open to interpretation. It can be contested, even, as happened in Salonica after the war, in a court of law. We should be wary of drawing too rigid a line between fact and interpretation, knowing that the process of narration is itself one of selection, organization and interpretation. But there is a line. Some things happened; others did not. Leon Batis and Albert Menasche were right: the Shoah is ultimately beyond human imagination. Every life lost was a world extinguished: the sheer scale of the event makes it inconceivable. Since Hannah Arendt coined her complicated idea about the banality of evil, the Shoah has become very familiar: too familiar for many. Not another book about the Holocaust ... It can seem, as the last witnesses die and memory becomes history, as everyone and their dog wants their say about this past, that evil is indeed being made banal. We are in danger of thinking that we *do* understand the Shoah, that it *is* conceivable, that our human imagination can indeed compass its truths. The value of the witnesses, the value of Isaac Matarasso's words, is that they are still shocking.

There are always stories. They are how each generation passes on what matters to the next. They are passed from one hand to the next, small suitcases, containing treasures. In this way one generation's memories are inherited by the next. They change in that transmission but, as Elie Wiesel says, whoever listens to a witness becomes a witness. It is how we learn, as people and as a species. If we have not yet learned to manage our fear, our hatred or our greed, it is because we have not cared enough about what our parents and grandparents have told us.

Notes

1 I, Matarasso. *Ki ómos óloi tous den péthanan . . . I katastrofí ton Ellinoevraíon tis Thessaloníkis katá ti germanikí katochí* (Athens: Ekdóseis Alexandreia, 2018).

2 A translation of the 1948 Greek text was included, without the family's involvement, in S, Bowman. *The Holocaust in Salonika: Eyewitness Accounts*, translated by Isaac Benmayor (New York: Sephardic House, 2002).

3 The statistics were added in 1947, as they became available; the Epilogue alone is dated 1948.

4 The central text, written in French, was published in Greek (though it is not clear whether the text was translated by IM or by someone else), in seven successive issues of the weekly newspaper *Jewish Tribune (Israelitikon Vema)*. The series was headed 'The History of the Extermination of a People: The Persecution of the Jews of Thessaloniki. From the Journal of our Co-Religionist M.'. The first part was published on 1 March 1946, in issue 14, and the last on 19 April 1946, in issue 21.

5 Postcard to Andrée, August 1914.

6 The ship may have been the *Bosforo*, an Italian steamer bound for Salonica, sunk by submarine U-28 off the coast of Sardinia on 12 January 1918.

7 To Vidal Nahoum, in E, Morin. *Vidal et les Siens* (Paris: 1989). Vidal's son would become the eminent French intellectual Edgar Morin.

8 M, Molho. (ed.) *In Mémoriam : Hommage aux Victimes Juives des Nazies en Grèce* (Salonica: The Jewish Community of Salonica, 1948, 2nd edn 1988), p. 26.

9 Particular thanks must go to Dimitrios Varvaritis, who made available his inventory of IM's publications. Collated through painstaking archival research, this includes not only publications in professional journals such as the *Annales des maladies*

vénériennes but also, of greater historical importance, the articles about the Shoah in Salonica that appeared in Jewish publications (in Greek and in French) between 1946 and 1961.

10   RM memoir, 1981–82.

11   See below, 'In Memory of Dr Joseph Amariglio', p. 188.

12   IM, letter to PM, 15 December 1956.

13   See below, 'In Memory of Dr Joseph Amariglio', p. 188.

14   The organization of this public humiliation on the Sabbath and in a square named Liberty was characteristic of German procedures throughout the occupied territories. Itzchak Nechama, who suffered on that day, lived to give evidence about it at the trial of Adolf Eichmann in Jerusalem on 22 May 1961. He testified that: 'An order had been given to form lines without moving, and the sun was very strong and the Jews were not able to stand in the sun for a long time; but they were so slow making the arrangements, that many could not stand it. They also wanted to have fun, they did it for laughs. When they were in a certain row, an SS policeman would come and push them away and start hitting and fooling around. And at the windows there were Germans taking photos of them and applauding. [. . .] If you could have seen me on Saturday at 2.30, the state I was in after these exercises, the blows I got, why – I do not know. I did not do anything to them. I did not owe them anything, and in the end they gave me a bloody thrashing. And not only me, but my family also. [. . .] They took me and beat me and organised all kinds of exercises, and after that there were more beatings and more. And then I was taken to a doctor. If I were in Salonika now I could bring the doctor; he is alive and well – it is Dr Kopers. [. . .] The doctor was fetched and he treated me. I was sick for two weeks; for four days I was unconscious.' *The Trial of Adolf Eichmann, Record of Proceedings in the District Court of Jerusalem* vol. II (Jerusalem: State of Israel Ministry of Justice, 1992), pp. 852–3.

15   RM, memoir, 1981–82.

16   Part V, p. 226.

17   This was investigated during the research from the 2018 Greek edition of IM's book.

18   I, Dublon-Knebel. (ed.) *German Foreign Office Documents on the Holocaust in Greece (1937–1944)* (Tel-Aviv: Tel Aviv University, 2007), p. 151. (Information from Dimitrios Varvaritis.)

19　See Eleni, Beze. 'Dr Isaac Matarasso and his Multiple Contribution to the Post-War Reconstruction of the Jewish Communities in Greece', forthcoming in Greek. The article is part of Beze's research for a doctoral dissertation on 'Greek Jews after the Shoah: Issues of Memory and Identity', Department of History, University of Thessaly, Volos, Greece.

20　Ibid.

21　Ibid.

22　IM letter to RM and PM, 19 September 1955.

23　IM letter to RM, 5 January 1958; his last letter.

24　IM letter to PM, 15 December 1956.

25　Memory may be slipping here: there is an Impasse Berlioz in Toulouse, and a rue des Pénitents Blancs, but they are not connected.

26　In 1911 IM's Ottoman identity papers record that he speaks French, Turkish and German (though no mention is made of Ladino or Greek). German was a leading language of science, and IM may have acquired some knowledge as an aspiring medical student (as Primo Levi did as a chemistry student in 1930s Turin). But PM, who is a German-speaker, never heard him use the language after the war, and his interpretation of German words and proper names is not always accurate. (Nor are Polish place-names necessarily correct as spelt, but the underlying information is in almost all cases exact – he is a gold-standard witness.) The term 'Dienststelle', as used here, represents the generic word 'department', in the administrative sense. The Polish town Sosnowiec (here 'Sosnonie'), in Upper Silesia, had within its hinterland a population of 80,000 Jews before the German invasion of Poland in 1939. By the end of 1943 there were none left, and the methods employed in this wholesale destruction were of almost unbelievable brutality. There was indeed in Sosnowiec an important section or department of the 'Fremdvölkischen Arbeitseinsatz', the staff of which co-operated with the Gestapo in the extermination of Jews sent to Auschwitz and other camps in Poland, as well as in the organization of slave labour in these camps. The second-in-command was SS-Sturmbannführer Lindner, as given here, who liaised with his SS counterpart in Salonica.

27　Sicherheitsdienst, the Security Service of the SS, the major paramilitary organization of the Nazi state. Dieter Wisliceny,

SS-Hauptsturmführer, organized the deportation of Salonica's Jewish population in the space of three months.

28 Probably an acronym for *Zwangsarbeitlager*.

29 Laskaris Papanaoum, 'the city's most notorious antisemite': see M, Mazower. *Inside Hitler's Greece* (London: Yale University Press, 1993), p. 207.

30 See 'The Wireless', p. 207.

31 Between May and August 1941 a unit made up of Wehrmacht officers and academics, known as the Rosenberg Kommando, looted synagogues, archives and libraries throughout Greece (Mazower as cited in no 29 above, p. 237).

32 Called on by the King to take over the government at a time of unrest in 1936, the royalist and nationalist General Metaxas remained in power until his death on the eve of the German occupation, leaving the country deeply divided.

33 As a doctor, IM will have had immediate experience of the famine, though less among his regular clients than at the free clinics he ran in one of the poor districts of the city. His son, Robert, writes of women and children begging for food in the more prosperous streets where the family lived. Few doors, he adds, were opened to them. This famine was quite indiscriminate: the Germans believed in living off the countries they occupied.

34 Kraft durch Freude was an organization set up in 1933 as a propaganda tool to promote National Socialism to the German people and tourism to visitors. During the war it supplied entertainment to the troops serving in occupied countries.

35 Schutzpolizei, or German State Police, affiliated to the SS.

36 This concession covered IM, his wife and his son: see p. 39.

37 David, IM's younger brother, escaped from the city with his wife, Rachel, and children Ninon and Henri. Separated during the journey to Athens, Rachel and Ninon were captured by German forces in the countryside but escaped with the help of Greek villagers. The family lived in hiding in the capital for two years, moving from one place to another. When Rachel died of illness, she was buried according to Christian rites. David and the children eventually escaped to Turkey by boat.

38 Among those on this first Transport was IM's father, Aaron: see pp. 42 and 231.

39 IM attributes this passage to Léon Dubnov, but may have meant the Russian Jewish writer and historian Simon Dubnow (1860–1941).

40 Vital Hasson, who escaped from the concentration camp in August 1943, during the last days of the deportation period, was arrested, tried and condemned to death in July 1946. In October 1947 he was still alive, in prison in Corfu; he was executed in March 1948.

41 At a special meeting held on 11 September 1945, the reconstituted Council of the Jewish Community of Salonica passed a resolution calling for the prosecution of 53 named collaborators, including Koretz, Uziel, Albala and Hasson, and requesting its lawyers to begin proceedings. First on the list of named witnesses ready to testify against them is 'Isaac Matarasso, doctor, 93 Tsimiski Street'.

42 Bergen-Belsen, a military training area in Lower Saxony, was used as a prisoner-of-war camp from 1939. In April 1943 part of the site was designated as a holding camp for Jewish prisoners who were intended to be exchanged for prisoners in other countries or for hard currency. The last Jews transported from Salonica in August 1943 were 'privileged' in being held as de facto hostages rather than being sent to the extermination and work camp at Auschwitz-Birkenau like everyone else. In April 1945 Bergen-Belsen was the first camp to be liberated by the British Army: their discovery of 60,000 sick and starving inmates and 13,000 unburied corpses was a first sight of the horror of the concentration camp system and made Belsen's name notorious in the English-speaking world. The idea that anyone brought here could be considered privileged is heartbreaking.

43 IM does not mention that, in the face of this understandable hostility, he argued for treating these survivors like all other members of the community, holding to his Hippocratic oath of providing help universally to the sick.

44 A slip of the pen here: there were in fact no Transports between 1 June and 13 August, the date of the final Transport.

45 RM's notes, though incomplete, suggest that it was this unit that was responsible for his arrest and that of his father in the summer of 1943.

46 A record of Rebecca Franco, *née* Pissirilo, is held by the United States Holocaust Memorial Museum, which includes the

information in IM's account, with some additional details. See: https://encyclopedia.ushmm.org/content/en/id-card/rebecca-pissirilo

47 Fofo Esrati is named later in the typescript as Fofo Eskenazi. This is probably a moment of inattention in IM's part, as the name Elie Eskenazi figures just before the last on the list; it has been corrected in accordance.

48 The Louis d'or was a solid gold coin issued, with interruptions, between 1640 and 1914 by the French state. It is hard to calculate what its value might have been in Salonica at the time, but in France it was worth 3,000 to 4,000 francs in 1944. IM clearly implies that these lives were bought at a very high ransom.

49 These men are referred to on coming pages as Kapos. Often former convicts or political prisoners, picked for their potential for brutality, they were used by the SS to enforce discipline and keep the camps running, while being motivated by a mixture of fear and privileges.

50 Mr Cohen seems to have been deported from Salonica on 3 or 5 April 1943 (he says it was 4 April, but there was no train that day). The Greek State Railways reported that each of these Transports included 2,800 people, so whether he or IM was mistaken in reporting a figure of 2,700 is unknown. In any case, the total he gives for those assigned to work and those sent immediately to their deaths amounts to only 2,480 people. The discrepancy probably represents those who died during the long journey to Auschwitz-Birkenau.

51 These words were placed at the entrance of many concentration camps, including Auschwitz, and are commonly rendered as 'Work sets you free'. What IM's text has here is, in capitals, LE TRAVAIL PROCURE LA JOIE, or 'Work brings joy'. No prisoner who had been at Auschwitz could possibly make this mistake. IM typed in French words he heard spoken in unfamiliar German during an evening of Greek (and probably Ladino). If he gives the slogan only in French, it is probably because he wasn't sure of the spelling. On p. 87 above, he quotes in German another slogan, at the time much better known, 'Kraft durch Freude' ('Strength through Joy'). It seems that he confused the adjectives 'frei' = 'free' and 'froh' = 'happy/joyful', which sound very similar, and thought he had heard 'Arbeit macht freu', which indeed would have meant 'Le travail procure la joie'. Nowadays

the Auschwitz slogan is well known and often quoted, the other largely forgotten.

52 Jaworzno concentration camp was established in 1943 and operated until January 1945.

53 'The collaborator Pericles Nikolaides was handed over four formerly Jewish-owned cafés in order to set up gambling dens and casinos and bought up the Baron Hirsch quarter, now "silent and deserted", before demolishing it and selling off the rubble at a handsome profit.' See M, Mazower. *Salonica, City of Ghosts, Christians, Muslims and Jews, 1430–1950* (London: Harper Collins, 2004), p. 448.

54 'Laskaris Papanaoum, who later lived quietly in retirement in West Germany, was rewarded for his help in rounding up Jews in hiding by being given the largest tannery in the Balkans.' Mazower as cited in no 53 above, p. 448.

55 J, Plaut. *Greek Jewry in the Twentieth Century, 1913–1983: Patterns of Jewish Survival in the Greek Provinces before and after the Holocaust* (Cranbury, NJ: Associated University Presses, 1996) p. 59.

56 Data collected in July 1946; see Bowman (2002), as cited in no 2 above, p. 174.

57 The figure of 2,200 Jews in Salonica in November 1947 is probably an overestimate; in his report about the situation of Jewish communities in Greece dated June 1947, IM had estimated the Jewish community of Salonica as numbering 1,800.

58 It is not clear how or by whom these percentages were calculated, and since they add up to more than 100 per cent, they cannot be considered precise. But the assessment that 40 per cent of survivors were without means of support, and another 50 per cent were struggling to survive without aid, is probably accurate enough.

59 IM doesn't mention it, but it was the *Jewish Tribune* (*Israelitikon Vema*) that first published his Greek articles on the Shoah.

60 The EAM (Ethnikó Apeleftherotikó Métopo, or National Liberation Front) was the principal organized Resistance group in Greece during the Second World War, led by the Greek Communist Party but involving other leftist groups. Both Isaac and Robert owed their survival to its military arm, ELAS (Ellinikós Laïkós Apeleftherotikós Stratós, or Greek People's Liberation Army), which dominated military resistance to the German occupation of Macedonia.

61 For further details about the difficulties faced by Jewish survivors, see Mazower, as cited in no 53 above, pp. 449–58.

62 The Joint, as it was known, was the American Joint Distribution Committee, which provided vital relief to Jews in Europe during and after the war. 'The central board of Jewish communities concentrated on the reclamation of individual, communal, and heirless property, while the American Joint Distribution Committee (AJDC) helped individuals reconstitute their family and work life, whether in Greece or overseas. The Central Board depended on the AJDC, not only for monetary support in the rehabilitation process, but also for the international political leverage it could exert on the Greek government.' (Plaut, as cited in no 55 above, p. 75.)

63 Three pieces were published in 1959, in vol. 18 of *Le Judaïsme Séphardi*: 'Mordoh Pitchon, Teacher', 'Harbi Haïm Habib' and 'The Liberation'. They were accompanied by a moving obituary: 'The author of this account, Doctor Isaac Matarasso, a graduate of Toulouse University, died in Athens, at the age of 65, on 21 January 1958. He played an important role in the Jewish Community of Salonica, especially through his work after the Liberation of Greek territory. He was one of the most sympathetic figures in Greek Jewry, where he was held in high esteem and great affection, for the reliability of his scientific knowledge, for his goodness, for his disinterestedness and for his care of all the unfortunate and the disinherited of life. He reported diverse findings to the Academy of Medicine in Paris, and wrote a substantial work in Greek entitled ". . . And Yet Not All Died. . .", as important as it is moving, on the deportation of Salonica's Jews.' The same year, 'Life in the Ghetto' appeared in *Le Monde Juif* (vol. 16), also with an obituary whose similarity suggests it was written by the same hand. In 1961 the fifth and third pieces ('In memory of Dr Joseph Amariglio' and 'At the Headquarters of the SD, 42 Velissariou Street') were published in vol. 21 of *Le Judaïsme Séphardi*. It is not known who passed the texts to the publications, but the tone of the obituaries suggests that it may have been a friend and colleague, wishing to mark IM's memory by sharing papers that had been given to him. The appearance of the two final pieces in 1961, also in *Le Judaïsme Séphardi*, may be associated with the death of Andrée in September that year.

64 The association of former students of the Alliance Israélite Universelle schools made a lively contribution to Salonica's pre-war cultural life. IM, who owed the Alliance his education and thus his profession, was an active member with many friends in this circle.

65 These names are pseudonyms used by RM.

66 The 2nd SS Panzer Division 'Das Reich' became notorious for its war crimes, including the massacre of 642 civilians at Oradour-sur Glane in France on 10 June 1944.

67 This date depends on establishing a correlation between the accounts of father and son. IM reports as follows: 'However, around 15 March 1943 it was learned in the ghetto that three Jews married to German Aryans had been exempted from wearing the yellow badge and could live outside the ghetto. A few days later this favour was extended to other Jews married to Aryans'. See above, p. 39. Central to Robert's minutely detailed account of the days and hours immediately preceding their departure from the ghetto is the first deportation, its emotional shock compounded by the loss of his grandfather Aaron. This occurred indisputably on 15 March and left on all – father, mother and son – an indelible mark. In Robert's memory the visit to the Walbergs, the deportation and the visits of Father Katz to arrange their departure took place on successive days. So clear is his account, so specific and interlocked are events and times, that it remains persuasive.

68 See Introduction, p. 38.

69 See Introduction, p. 38 ff.

70 Elie Wiesel's remarks at the closing session of the International Conference 'The Legacy of Holocaust Survivors' at Yad Vashem's Valley of the Communities, April 2002: https://www.yadvashem.org/yv/en/exhibitions/wiesel/index.asp

71 'The records of Auschwitz-Birkenau show that 48,974 Jews arrived there from northern Greece; of these, 37,386 were immediately gassed. Hardly any of the remainder returned home' (Mazower, as cited in no 29 above, p. 244).

72 Nazi race ideology categorized individuals according to the number of their Jewish grandparents: anyone with three such relatives (defined by their enrolment in a Jewish congregation) was a Jew. A person with one or two Jewish grandparents was

a *Mischling* in the first or second degree. The pseudoscientific nature of this classification often made little difference to how people were treated. See S, Friedländer. *Nazi Germany and the Jews* (London: Weidenfeld & Nicolson, 1997), p. 148.

73 A, Menasche. *Birkenau (Auschwitz II), Memoirs of an Eye-Witness: How 72,000 Greek Jews Perished* (New York, 1947), p. 27. Dr Menasche was an important early witness to Nazi crimes; I believe that his book is an English translation of a text written in French but since lost. (This also accounts for the different spellings of his name.)

74 Following their arrest in the summer of 1943, Isaac and Robert were moved from the SD cellars in Velissariou Street to the city prison in the old Heptapyrgion fortress overlooking the city. Since it was administered by Greeks rather than Germans, it was possible for the Resistance to find sympathizers among the guards and secure the escape of the doctor they needed and the son they did not need but without whom he refused to go.

75 'Share your bread with the hungry' (Isaiah 58:7). This translation, from the Greek, was kindly provided by Rena Molho, who informs me that the abbreviation ETP signifies 'École spéciale des travaux publics, du bâtiment et de l'Industrie', founded in Paris in 1891. At the time of the building's construction, much of the centre of Salonica was being rebuilt under the direction of the French architect and urbanist Ernest Hébrard, following a catastrophic fire in 1917. Henri Alberto was the second child born to Isaac and Andrée, who died at or shortly after birth.

76 'En 1941, elle [Matanoth Laevionim] eut à sa tête Aaron Matarasso, un homme modeste et bon, dont la vie fut consacrée en grande partie au bien public, sans ostentation ni gloriole. En dépit de son âge très avancé, cet homme de grande vertu fut déporté en Pologne et dirigé vers le crematorium, à sa descente du train à Birkenau.' Molho as cited in no 8 above, p. 25.

77 Menasche, as cited in no 72 above, p. 7.

78 B, Schlink. *Guilt about the Past* (London: University of Queensland Press, 2009).

Note on the authors

Dr Isaac Matarasso was born in Salonica in 1892, when the city was part of the Ottoman Empire. He studied medicine at the University of Toulouse, and published his thesis in 1917. He practised in Salonica until his arrest in 1943, and organised health services for the Jewish survivors after the German withdrawal. He moved to Athens in 1946, with his wife Andrée and son Robert, where he resumed medical practice until his death in 1958.

Robert Matarasso was born in Salonica in 1927, and survived the Occupation partly with his parents and partly alone. He left Greece in 1948 and after agriculture studies in France, came to England with his wife Pauline in 1956, where he farmed until his death in 1982.

Pauline Matarasso studied at Oxford University and the Sorbonne in Paris before marrying Robert Matarasso in 1952. She has translated books for Penguin Classics among others and written on literature and history.

François Matarasso is a community artist and writer; his latest book, *A Restless Art*, was published in 2019.

Note on the type

The text of this book is set in Minion, a digital typeface designed by Robert Slimbach in 1990 for Adobe Systems. The name comes from the traditional naming system for type sizes, in which minion is between nonpareil and brevier. It is inspired by late Renaissance-era type.